ADVANCE PRAISE

"Feeling ever more stuck in the status quo? Exhausted from trying to drag your team toward the goal line? Ready to leave industrial-era images of leadership behind and shift into a twenty-first-century mindset? If the answer to any or all of those questions is yes, then Bill Flynn's fine new book is for you! From his decades of progressive business coaching, Bill shares insights on how to shift into effective team focus, how to design collaborative systems that work for everyone in your organization, and how to help focus the whole team on the importance of cash in creating a healthy construct in which everyone involved comes out ahead! A fine read for any leader of the future!"

—ARI WEINZWEIG, CO-FOUNDING PARTNER OF
ZINGERMAN'S COMMUNITY OF BUSINESSES
AND AUTHOR OF *ZINGERMAN'S GUIDE TO
GOOD LEADING (PARTS 1, 2, 3, AND 4)*

"Finally! A book that boils down the overabundance of leadership guidance and business systems into the few foundational things you need to get started. Bill has a talent for boiling down complex concepts to their essence and sharing them crisply and concisely—making them easy to understand and take action on immediately. Further, Faster is no different—leaders will enjoy this useful book."

—SHANNON SUSKO, AWARD-WINNING ENTREPRENEUR AND COACH, BEST-SELLING AUTHOR, RECOGNIZED AS ONE OF CANADA'S 150 WOMEN

"I have known Bill Flynn for many years as a coach of successful entrepreneurs. He has more than thirty years of experience working for and advising hundreds of companies. In the world of business, he has done it all, growing companies from startups to successful outcomes, IPOs, or acquisitions.

"He is a sought-after speaker within the business community, with a wealth of knowledge and experience. Like Bill, this book is well-thought-out, insightful, and full of wisdom. His writing is like his coaching, providing help to business leaders with straightforward and practical advice, and tools to solve their problems."

—DAVE BANEY, BUSINESS COACH AND AUTHOR OF *THE 3X5 COACH*

"*Growing a business is a team sport, and no one knows that better than author and coach Bill Flynn. Further, Faster is the one book you need to get now to help you and your team (and your company) grow.*"

—ELIZABETH CROOK, CEO OF ORCHARD ADVISOR AND AUTHOR OF *LIVE LARGE: THE ACHIEVER'S GUIDE TO WHAT'S NEXT*

"*In Further, Faster, Bill Flynn has successfully synthesized the wisdom he has gained from 30 years of work experience and the hundreds of books he has read on business management, leadership, team building, and neuroscience. Bill's style is direct and punchy. His concepts are right on! He provides lots of practical business wisdom that is of value to leaders of businesses of all sizes. Every entrepreneur should read this book, especially if they want to go further, faster!*"

—KEN ESTRIDGE, SPEAKER, BUSINESS GROWTH EXPERT, AND AUTHOR OF *INSPIRE ACCOUNTABILITY*

"*If you wish to run your business in a 'healthy and thriving' way, Further, Faster is a must-read for you. Included is the 'Further, Faster Checklist,' which will become your top-10 to-do list. Some books provide insight and understanding—others explain how. Further, Faster does both!*"

—HARLAN GEISER, FORMER CEO, BUSINESS COACH, AND EOS IMPLEMENTER

"*Many of us know that what got you here (the success you've demonstrated so far) will not get you there (the keys to success ahead). But how many of us know how to get there? Bill's book and framework for growth are like AI-powered thinking for humans. He takes the guesswork out of growth and tells it uniquely to the fast-growth startup company. Having scaled many startup businesses, Bill's further, faster technology and coaching for fast-growth companies is a go-to resource for the next generation of leaders.*"

—JONATHAN GOLDHILL, EXIT COACH AND AUTHOR
OF *DISRUPTIVE SUCCESSOR* AND *SCALE UP*

FURTHER, FASTER

BILL FLYNN

FURTHER, FASTER

THE VITAL FEW STEPS
THAT TAKE THE
GUESSWORK
OUT OF GROWTH

LIONCREST
PUBLISHING

FURTHER, FASTER

The Vital Few Steps That Take the Guesswork out of Growth

ISBN   978-1-5445-0783-5 *Paperback*

978-1-5445-0782-8 *Ebook*

978-1-5445-0784-2 *Audiobook*

To my family, with pride,
and to all those exceptional leaders who
make the world a better place.

CONTENTS

INTRODUCTION

"Worldwide, there are about 300 million persons trying to start about 150 million businesses [at any given time]. About one third will be launched, so you can assume 50 million new firm births per year. Or about 137,000 per day."[1]

That's right: About 6,000 new companies start every hour of every day, year after year, according to research compiled by the late research consultant Moya K. Mason. She then goes on to note that firm "birth and death" rates are about equal, with roughly 120,000 active firms terminating trading each day. And it's not getting any better, even for more established firms. Four hundred and forty firms that were listed within the Fortune 500 in 1955 have

---

[1]   Moya K. Mason, "Research on Small Businesses," *MKM Research*, http://www.moyak.com/papers/small-business-statistics.html#targetText=About%20one%20third%20will%20be,Or%20about%20137%2C000%20per%20day.&targetText=Among%20this%202.4%20billion%2C%20about,initial%20three%20years%20of%20operation.

been replaced as of 2017. According to Credit Suisse, the average age of an S&P 500 company is fewer than twenty years, down from sixty years in the 1950s.[2]

So many new businesses begin, yet so few remain in the short term—or the long run. No doubt, their founders all started out with hopeful visions of success. Yet they faltered.

It's time to take a step back and ask, "What's going on?"

This is what I do every day in my work as a business coach. Because what I've found is that no one talks about what *really* works. They talk about what's worked for them, which is almost always a unique situation. They rely on conventional wisdom—or their own intuition. With this book, I want to introduce you to what's worked across thousands of businesses over a long period of time. Few business owners and leaders know the rare things that exceptional companies consistently do well and that have been proven to be effective. The lessons aren't taught in business school. They're seldom shared among leaders. This creates a mismatch between what science knows and what business does.

---

2   Michael Sheetz, "Technology killing off corporate America: Average life span of companies under 20 years," *CNBC*, August 24, 2017, https://www.cnbc.com/2017/08/24/technology-killing-off-corporations-average-lifespan-of-company-under-20-years.html.

The problems that plague businesses aren't felt only by founders and leaders—they extend to the whole workforce. According to Gallup and research and survey consortium Mayflower Group, more than half of our team members are disengaged, too many actively.[3] Can you imagine relying on dozens, hundreds, or thousands of disengaged people to help make your business a success? This is where many companies are at today.

Why do people show up at work (and for that matter, in life) this way? Because it's what we were taught by our parents, peers, teachers, and other influencers.

Author and Harvard professor Amy Edmondson offers this explanation:

> It turns out that no one wakes up in the morning, jumps out of bed and says, "I can't wait to get to work today to look ignorant, incompetent, intrusive, or negative." On average, we prefer to look smart, helpful, and positive. The good news/bad news about all this is that it's very easy to manage. Don't want to look ignorant, don't ask questions. Don't want to look incompetent, don't admit your weakness or mistake. Don't want to look intrusive, don't offer

3   "State of the American Workplace," *Gallup*, https://news.gallup.com/reports/178514/state-american-workplace.aspx.

ideas and if you don't want to look negative, by all means, don't criticize the status quo.[4]

We're taught to "go with the flow" from an early age, and by the time we become adults, we've perfected the behavior. Simon Sinek, renowned author, motivational speaker, and marketing consultant calls this our second job at work—the job of lying, hiding, and faking in order to feel "safe." And it's killing productivity on many levels, virtually destroying any chance of taking a business further, faster.

HOW DID WE GET HERE?

No entrepreneur starts out this way. Think back to when you made the decision to start your business. Maybe you were tired of working for someone else. Maybe you got sick of settling for mediocrity and thought you could do better calling all the shots. *Something* drove you to cut the "employee cord" and risk a lot on your own skills. You must have felt strongly about what you wanted to bring to the world and had a lot of confidence in your abilities and potential. Think back to what being a business owner was like then, versus what it's like for you now.

---

4   Pangambam S (transcriber), "*Building a Psychologically Safe Workplace: Amy Edmondson (Transcript),*" September 8, 2019, https://singjupost.com/ building-a-psychologically-safe-workplace-amy-edmondson-transcript/.

How did we get here?

When you start a business, it's just you and maybe a couple of other people. So you care about only a few things and focus on just three constituencies: (1) your employees, (2) your customers, and (3) your market. You're very close to those constituencies. You hire, and train, and sit with these people; answer the phone; and close the deals. You go to conferences and network with people to see where the industry's going and what the market's doing. You do all those things to get your business off the ground, and guess what? It works. After a year or so, you've got a real business. And it grows.

But as your business grows, you start to move away from those constituencies. Someone else is doing all the hiring, and they're not always making the best choices. Since you don't deal with employee issues anymore, people who shouldn't be there linger on. You don't know what's going on with your customers, either, because you have salespeople, customer support people, and tech support people for that—and they don't tell you everything. Your marketing people attend the conferences for you and report back, telling you what they think you want to know about what they saw and heard.

You're that person in the office who no one wants to disturb or upset. You don't have the kind of information you used to get when you started the company, and most of what you do get is second-hand. You seldom get bad news, and you have to wonder if everything's really going that well—or if people aren't telling you everything.

So if you're not paying attention to your employees, customers, and the market, what are you paying attention to? Your calendar must be empty. Except it's not, because the bigger you get, the more you take on that doesn't really matter. You get involved in the decisions that aren't going to save your business, never mind grow it.

If you don't believe me, take a look at your calendar right now. Look at how you're spending your week. Are you guiding the most important decisions that will grow your business, or filling your time with things that don't matter? When your job is to grow the business, pretty much anything that doesn't contribute to that doesn't matter. That includes chasing revenue, by the way.

Do I have your attention yet?

MIND READER

I look forward to the day when entrepreneurs and business owners do their jobs differently. I want them to spring out of bed every morning, eager to make a difference in the lives of their raving fans—their customers. I want them to end each workday knowing their employees are leaving the office happy and fulfilled, looking forward to coming back to work the next day, instead of living for the weekend.

I'm working toward that day when every business leader is so close to his customers, they believe he can read their minds. A day when every business leader understands exactly what her customers are trying to accomplish as she addresses their key struggles—while also making their lives easier, more enjoyable, and more productive.

I am committed to the day when every leader can predict their business metrics and customer preferences years in advance with startling accuracy. The key is not to be a great "guesser," but to *intentionally commit time and attention to a few important long-term decisions and actively manage a system for predicting these metrics and preferences within the business process.* The most successful leaders create their future! Barring impactful unexpected events, I believe this is achievable because I have seen it.

Years ago, I took on a consulting client who was looking to sell his business. "Make me look as big as you possibly can," he told me. I created a sales process, hired a team, and within a year, the business was purchased by a much larger, IT services organization for a good amount of money. Within a few months, the original owner moved on while I stayed to run the division. In my first days as general manager, we suffered a serious hardware issue that resulted in a massive meltdown in services. One of our most critical services—email delivery—ground to a halt. This was before Amazon web services, when businesses just rented server space at third-party sites. The company accelerated rehabbing the data infrastructure but we still lost a thousand customers in a week. The president of the company and I visited with customers and partners to try and keep them on board. These weren't trivial partners either; they were hundreds-of-million-dollar-if-not-billion-dollar partners. By comparison, we were small potatoes.

We had to do something drastic if we were going to get our customers back on board. We couldn't just patch it up and hope for the best. I had a vision for the company, and I wanted the network people to see it too.

"Five nines," I told them, "is what we're shooting for. We need—at a minimum—a 99.999 percent uptime." I also created a scoring system to gauge our customer's loyalty (this was also before Net Promoter), and the results were not good: 2.9 out of 5, or 58 percent. I added to the vision: "We need a score of four out of five—80 percent—from our customers." I really wanted 4.5 out of 5, but I didn't want to overwhelm the team at this point. I knew what I wanted to see but I didn't know how to get there. The network team could figure it out, I believed, but they needed support from leadership. I told them, "You know what I want. You have to build the map to get us there and tell me what you need to build it."

I wanted the team to commit to something they could visualize—something bigger than themselves. I created rewards and recognitions around the 80 percent goal. We initiated "Spark" as a way to recognize people, which I'll talk about in a lot more detail later in this book. It took us a while, but eighteen months later when I left the company, we had achieved and maintained a score of 4.6 in customer loyalty—92 percent! Even more, at about the ten-month mark, I knew we were going to do great things as my operating job was over by 11 a.m. each day. I now had time to focus on the future.

When I came into the business, it had been around for seven years and was doing $9 million in revenue. I left it at $14 million. Not bad for two years' work. And we did it without hiring a bunch of new people. The key was to have that vision and paint that picture for the people who could make it happen. Then get behind them, support them, and reward them for working together as a team to get there.

The goals I set for my team—and the ones I'm asking you to set for yours—aren't a stretch at all. They are totally within reach: I want every leader's team to truly act like a team, each member willing to sacrifice his individual needs for the greater good. Each member trusting her fellow team members to do their jobs, and when she's struggling, to have her back. Every single person on every team knowing they can come to work and never have to worry about anyone undermining them, directly or indirectly.

If this is the kind of workplace you've already built, then you don't need my book. Feel free to pass it on to a friend—I won't be offended. But if it sounds like something you're longing for, keep reading.

BILL THE STARTUP GUY

I've been a student of business for three decades. In the 1990s, I was a "startup guy," working in sales and marketing for new businesses where I talked to customers and partners all day. I loved it, and by 2015, I'd worked with ten startups that ended with two IPOs and seven acquisitions, achieving a 50 percent success rate. And five out of six of these successes were achieved from 1991 through 2011!

Being something of an etiologist, I naturally want to know the cause of every effect, specifically as it applies to business and why some succeed, yet many fail. Outside the workplace, I studied everything I could get my hands on from people who ran businesses—people like Jim Collins, Michael Porter, Pat Lencioni, Peter Drucker, and more. Digging deep into what they had to teach me, along with what I had learned on my own, I discovered the reasons most businesses don't last aren't really that complicated or many when you get down to it.

Once I'd distilled this knowledge down to the basics, I took my skills on the road, helping leaders figure out how to run their businesses in a healthy and thriving way. As a business coach, I've helped leaders fire themselves from the day-to-day so they can focus much more time on the three key elements that drive healthy and sustainable growth: team, strategy and execution, and cash.

Alan Mulally, arguably the finest CEO in the last fifty to one hundred years, wonderfully exemplifies these principles. Mulally helped turn Boeing around in the middle of 9/11—then did the same with Ford during the Great Recession. I am unaware of any business leader who not only survived two existential, economic crises, but also whose failing businesses came out of these crises even stronger. The book *American Icon* tells the story of Mulally's strategy at Ford; the three key items of Team, Strategy/Execution system, and Cash are highlighted:

- Aggressively restructure to operate profitably at the

current demand and changing model mix. (EXECU-TION)
- Accelerate development of new products our customers want and value. (STRATEGY)
- Finance our plan and improve our balance sheet. (CASH)
- Work together effectively as one team. (PEOPLE AND TEAMS)[5]

These are the same principles I teach as a business coach. Many leaders and businesses need guidance and support in this respect. To assist more leaders, I took the best of what I know and created a foundation that anyone can apply—the vital steps to take that will move you further, faster and take the guesswork out of growth.

PREDICTING YOUR COMPANY'S GROWTH

Business growth happens in stages, and the initial stage eventually slows and begins to decline. This process may take years or longer, but the eventuality is a constant. In order to overcome the decline, the leadership team must figure out the next growth curve as quickly as it is feasible to do so.

This process starts by firing yourself from running the

---

5   Bryce G. Hoffman, *American Icon: Alan Mulally and the Fight to Save Ford Motor Company* (New York: Crown, 2012).

company and spending more and more time on predicting the future. Leaders must create space and time to think about what's next. The time it takes to figure this out varies, so you should start as soon as the current business begins to scale. At that point, your job is no longer primarily working *in* the business, but to spend more time working *on* the business.

The bottom line is that the best leaders focus relentlessly on the following:

Spending *less* time managing the present; spending *more* time predicting the future.

Predicting Your Company's Growth Curves

Your job as head of company is to define
your future growth curve.

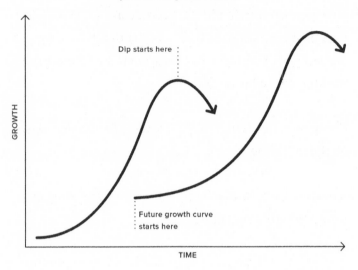

Once you've begun to scale, your #1 priority as the head of the company is predicting your company's next growth curve.

An example of a business that successfully predicted growth curves is Apple. Once Steve Jobs righted the ship after being reinstated as CEO, he and the team began to look for the next big opportunity, which is where the iPod came from. Next was iTunes, followed by the iPhone, and so on. Apple is continuously working on the future. Amazon CEO Jeff Bezos speaks of similar planning where he and the team are two to three years ahead of the current quarter.

When people have the chance to think, they can easily discern between what's essential and what's not...We need to develop a routine that enables that space to think. In a world where we have so much information, we need more time to think and process it, not less.

—GREG MCKEOWN, *ESSENTIALISM*

The bottom line is that the best leaders focus relentlessly on the following: Spending *less* time managing the present; spending *more* time predicting the future.

A FRAMEWORK FOR GROWTH

In today's busier and busier world, you need more time, not less time, to make good decisions. This book will help you get there.

There are just a few things you need to do. Look at it as what Shannon Susko calls in her book *The Metronome Effect* a "growth framework."[6] The Growth Framework image illustrates the many facets of this framework, and your job is to do all these things. I'm not going to go into everything you see here; I'm going to pick the few key areas that I've seen get leaders and their businesses the furthest, fastest.

---

6   Shannon Byrne Susko, *The Metronome Effect: The Journey to Predictable Profit* (Charleston: Advantage, 2014).

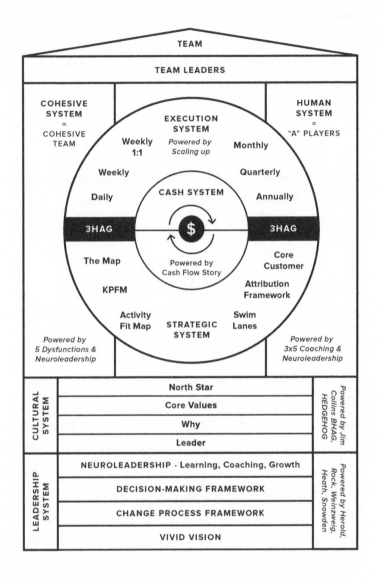

Think of your framework for growth as a "house" comprising seven subsystems: *Leadership, Cultural, Cohesive, Human, Execution, Strategic,* and *Cash.* Credit: Based on the Growth Framework by Shannon Susko

Like any good house, every good business has a solid foundation. A firm foundation is a cultural system comprising the Leader, the Why, the Core Values, and the North Star. The leader is you. The why is the reason or purpose for your business, and the core values are the rules you live and work by in the business—the immutable behaviors you expect from everyone, every day. The North Star is your company's long-term core destination, which Jim Collins calls the "BHAG™" or Big Hairy Audacious Goal. The foundation rests on good soil, beginning with what business consultant and author Cameron Herold calls your "Vivid Vision."[7]

As the leader, it's also your job to clearly communicate the future to your people so they can visualize it in the present. This is the vivid vision. Your people see it and see themselves in it, and then they decide whether they buy into that vision. Not all will, but team members who do will probably be more productive and more likely to rise to the ranks of A-player status. Anyone who doesn't buy into the vivid vision may want to leave the company and find employment at a company whose vivid vision aligns with theirs, and that will allow them to make the impact they want to make in the world.

On top of your vivid vision is the change process frame-

---

7 Cameron Herold, *Vivid Vision: A Remarkable Tool For Aligning Your Business Around a Shared Vision of the Future* (Austin: Lioncrest, 2018).

work. Change is usually haphazard and often fails. According to a Gallup article by David Leonard and Claude Coltea, more than 70 percent of all change initiatives fail.[8] However, having a managed process like Bottom Line Change™ from Ari Weinzweig, founder of Zingerman's Community of Business to shepherd the change process allows you to control change and be a change agent, instead of allowing change to happen. Then comes the decision-making framework, a managed process for making decisions, and finally, neuroleadership through learning, coaching, and growth.

Neuroleadership is understanding how the brain works—how connections are made, how the brain makes decisions, and how people learn. An organization that's growing in terms of revenue, profit, and cash is also growing in terms of its people's skills, capabilities, and knowledge. If you don't know how people learn, you will do what most leaders do, which is to get people in a room, tell them stuff, and send them back to work. That's not how people learn.

---

8   David Leonard and Claude Coltea, "Most Change Initiatives Fail – But They Don't Have To," *Business Journal*, May 24, 2013 https://news.gallup.com/businessjournal/162707/change-initiatives-fail-don.aspx.

When you give advice, there is no opportunity for the person to figure anything out. Instead, you can coach them to come to their own conclusions and allow them space to grow. This method results in knowledge that sticks and results in a better culture and a more cohesive team. You, as the leader, start the business and then you engage a cohesive team, represented by the walls of the house. Cohesive means that they fight in a healthy way. The right-hand wall is the human system, specifically your A-players, who are typically two to three times more productive than anyone else. A-players are key to your success, but they're often ignored because they don't seek nor need attention. They do not need to be managed; they live and breathe the culture and consistently exceed expectations. Other players on the team—especially the ones who complain the most—get the most attention.

When a business is in trouble, it's the A-players who leave first. They're in demand and can easily move on. Since we've been taking them for granted, they don't feel a need to stay. There is no loyalty and no connection to the business for an A-player who has been ignored.

Building a strong team requires creating a system where you pay attention to the A-players. You challenge them and give them opportunities to stretch their abilities. You also have to treat them like the humans they are, by recognizing and rewarding them.

You have B+ players who, with your support and encouragement, could become A-players, and you probably have B and C players too. First, focus on the A-players and make sure they're challenged. One way to do this is by handing them some of your work. This accomplishes another goal: getting some of the work off your plate so you can think about how to better run the business. Don't give them menial work—make sure it's work that stretches them and takes the fullest advantage of their strengths.

The top of the house is the team and the team leaders. The foundation, walls, and roof create the framework for your house, which is how you run the business on the inside. This is your execution system and your strategic system, which are connected. You start with a strategy, execute it, improve it, and repeat the cycle. Done well, you have the cash to run your business even better, make strategic bets, pay those A-players a little more, and take care of your teams.

GRAY MATTERS: A.G.E.S.

According to the NeuroLeadership Institute, the human brain remembers and processes information through a system known as A.G.E.S.: Attention, Generation, Emotion, and Spacing.[9] So to teach someone, you first have to get their *attention*. You do this by presenting something interesting or compelling, like a fun fact or engaging story. *Generation* refers to associating what you're teaching them to something that's meaningful to them. When I coach people, I say, "Here's what we're going to do. I'm going to teach you how to take your business further, faster." That gets their attention. Then I add, "If this could happen for you, take a minute to write down the impact that would have on your life." This allows them to decide what's important to them and connect it to what they're going to learn.

9   Weller, Chris, "The 4 Active Ingredients for Long-Term Learning," *NeuroLeadership*, April 30, 2019 https://neuroleadership.com/your-brain-at-work/ages-model-for-learning.

The next word in the A.G.E.S. acronym, *emotion*, is there because we learn better through emotion, whether positive, like love or happiness, or negative, like anger or sadness. We remember things that cause us to be emotional, though we remember the negative more readily than the positive as a function of survival, but any emotional connection we make improves our chances of learning. *Spacing* is the last part of A.G.E.S., which refers to learning over time. Cramming for a test doesn't allow your brain to recall knowledge as well as if you spaced out your learning. This is because when you access the same information regularly, your brain learns that the information is important and stores it in your long-term memory. This is why you can remember lyrics to songs from years ago.

In the following pages, we'll start with your people and more specifically, your teams. Without them, the rest of it won't happen.

But before we get into chapter 1, I've provided a checklist you can use to get a sense of where you and your team believe the company stands right now. The *Further, Faster Checklist* gauges each person's opinion on the current status of the business. It also provides insight into which parts of your organization need the most attention, so you can prioritize your actions.

After you've completed the checklist, we'll jump right into why performance is a team sport.

GET UP AND STRETCH: THE
FURTHER, FASTER CHECKLIST

Review the *Further, Faster Checklist* that follows before pro-
ceeding with this book. Then give each member of your team
a copy of the checklist or put it up on a board in a meeting, and
complete this simple exercise:

- Ask each team member to score each of the ten major items
  on the list with a score of 1 through 10, denoting the success
  with which each item is accomplished at your company.
- A score of "1" means the team member believes the company
  satisfies that item on the checklist very poorly, while a score
  of "10" denotes excellence.
- Once everyone's had a chance to provide their scores, add
  the scores for each item.
- Items with the lowest scores should be singled out as needing
  the most immediate attention from the team.

This is a quick and easy exercise that you can complete in a half
hour or so. Whether you have each team member record their
answers anonymously or openly is up to you; however, have each
person fill out their own checklist silently and separately. And
remember that each person's impression of how the company
is doing is important and deserves your attention.

Expect to be surprised. When I do this exercise with leadership
teams, it's usually an eye-opener. As leaders, we might think

everything's going well simply because we haven't asked if it isn't. But whatever the results, don't be discouraged. Instead, think of this as a starting point for you to measure your business against moving forward. Revisit the checklist regularly and ask your team to re-score it every quarter. You might be just as surprised by the progress that's possible!

Resources from this book, including the *Further, Faster Checklist*–plus bonus content–are available at *Further, Faster Resources*: https://catalystgrowthadvisors.com/catalyst-growth-advisors/further-faster-resources/.

THE FURTHER, FASTER CHECKLIST

1. **Cohesive Senior Leadership Team**

☐ Team members understand one another's differences, priorities, and styles (psychometrics applied; e.g., Predictive Index, DiSC).

☐ The team participates in ongoing, monthly, executive education (e.g. book, business summit, TED Talk, article).

☐ The team meets weekly for strategic thinking.

☐ The team "fights" in a healthy way. The "kind truth" is shared easily.

2. **Vivid Vision, Core Values, and Purpose are Clear and "Kept Alive"**

- ☐ The Head of Company has written a clear, comprehensive, and compelling Vivid Vision.
- ☐ All team members are crystal clear on the organization's BHAG (aka North Star, Core Destination).
- ☐ A handful of immutable behavioral rules (aka Core Values) are created and lived every day.
- ☐ The aforementioned are used to attract, hire, retain, grow, and exit team members.

3. **Team-First Culture: We Have a Deliberately Designed and Supported Team-Based Environment**

- ☐ The right team—with attention paid equally to each prospective member's cultural fit, skills, and knowledge within the team—is thoughtfully considered before building a key functional team and/or working a problem/opportunity.
- ☐ Each team is given what they need to succeed. Each team member is put in a position to maximize fit and take the fullest advantage of his/her natural talent and strengths in the role and for the team.
- ☐ All share a common goal as well as the rewards and responsibilities for goal achievement.
- ☐ Each will readily set aside individual and/or personal needs for the greater good of the group.

4. **We Have Created a Psychologically Safe Environment for All**

- Each team member feels secure to speak up, admit mistakes, or make errors without fear of scorn and/or ridicule.
- Each leader feels fully supported; promises—large and small—are kept by all, and nothing is shared inappropriately.
- We provide direction versus giving answers; we invite input for clarification and improvement; we create conditions for continued learning to achieve excellence; we value other team members as contributors with crucial knowledge and insight.

5. **Key Leader Strengths and Weaknesses are Known and Being Optimally Leveraged (Strengths) or Compensated for (Weaknesses)**
- Each leader completes a Love It/Loathe It process at least twice a year.
- Each leader has taken and discussed a Strengths-Finder (or similar) test.
- Each leader has created and discussed a growth development plan with his/her immediate superior.

6. **Strategy-Execution Rhythm (Intelligence System) is Established and Rigorously Followed**
- Scaling Up (or similar high-quality system) is established, followed, and measured consistently.
- The team meets regularly to update and validate the system's components.

☐ Every meeting is productive and moves the company forward.

7. **Each Team Member is Clear and Aligned on Key Fundamental Business Processes**
☐ Critical decision process framework
☐ Change implementation process
☐ Consistent "NeuroLeadership": brain-based learning, growth, and coaching plan that is mutually created, followed, and measured for all team members
☐ Critical decisions process is established and focused on achieving the best possible, timely outcome

8. **Suspect-to-Customer-to-Advocate Processes are Crafted and Practiced Regularly**
☐ Sales Playbook is created and leveraged by Sales and supporting teams.
☐ Weekly Sales Meeting agenda is created for continuous improvement in growth and forecasting.
☐ Customer Advocacy Playbook is created and leveraged by Customer Success and supporting teams.
☐ Weekly Customer Feedback Meeting agenda is created for continuous improvement in customer delight and business growth.

9. **Cash is King!**
☐ Weekly Cash Flow statement is provided to Head of Company.

- Working capital reserve is available for unexpected business fluctuations (two–twelve months, depending on the type of business you are in).
- "Profit Channel" is established to provide internal funding for future growth (e.g. 10–15 percent profit channel).
- Cash Conversion Cycle process is completed every six months at a minimum.

10. Enterprise Value Criteria are Established and Optimized

- The Entrepreneur/CEO/Owner is redundant in the business.
- Powerful, healthy Management Team/Bench is established for key positions.
- Revenue predictability and quality over several years, consistent growth in Revenue, Profit, and Cash
- Show significant growth potential in current, adjacent and/or new markets.
- Healthy team-based culture/High engagement organization

PART I

PERFORMANCE IS A TEAM SPORT

CHAPTER 1

CREATE A TEAM-BUILDING ENVIRONMENT

According to ADP Institute Research, in a survey of almost 20,000 people across nineteen countries, 83 percent of respondents stated that they are on at least one team, 64 percent of those people say they are on more than one team, and 75 percent of the respondents said the team they are on is not reflected in the org chart.

—MARCUS BUCKINGHAM (PARAPHRASED)[10]

From the 1940s through the '70s, the Ohio State Buckeyes were a collegiate powerhouse. This dominant football team won six national championships and numerous

---

10 Marcus Buckingham and Ashley Goodall, "The Power of Hidden Teams," *Harvard Business Review*, May 2019 https://hbr.org/cover-story/2019/05/the-power-of-hidden-teams.

conference championships—before running into a thirty-two-year drought.

In the 1960s, they started a tradition that may have contributed heavily to their downfall: awarding individual player performances after each game with stickers that were displayed on their helmets. For many decades, they gave players who performed well a sticker if they met certain benchmarks for performance, such as a quarterback throwing for a touchdown or a defensive player catching an interception. And in the 1980s and '90s, the team became less and less successful.

In 2000, Jim Tressel was hired as their new head coach. He noticed a pervasive sense of competitiveness and an emphasis on individual performance. Tressel recognized that for the team to be successful, people needed to be willing to make sacrifices for the good of the team. They needed to step back and compromise some of their own individual success for the team, as a whole, to win.

He came up with an ingenious change to the existing reward structure. After games, the individual Buckeye helmet sticker awards were replaced with team-based awards. He started giving Buckeye helmet stickers to the team unit when they met certain benchmarks. For example, when the offensive unit scored touchdowns or the defensive unit recorded an interception or recorded a sack, everybody on that unit would get a sticker.

Within two short years, Tressel completely turned the team around. They won the national championship in 2002 and again in 2014 under Urban Meyer, who continued the team-based award system. Every year since, with one exception, they have been consistently among the top ten teams in the country in one of the most competitive collegiate sports.

TEAMS MAKE IT HAPPEN

Football teams are very much like organizations. They have a complex hierarchical structure. There is a leader—a head coach—who is accountable to the athletic director and the fans. There is a large team of assistant coaches and trainers, and they're all involved in recruiting and building talent. Then, of course, there are the team members themselves.

Top business leaders are trying to manage the same dynamics in modern organizations. They are tasked with thinking about how to organize and cultivate a sense of group identity and enhanced team performance—a culture of belonging and team to drive the highest level of performance. Performance, after all, is a team sport.

So, there *is* a better way.

A football team may have some rock star players, but they succeed year after year because of the whole team. Likewise, businesses may rely on a handful of individuals—especially when they're small—but over time as they grow, they need teams to survive. Team performance almost always outweighs individual performance over the long term—and top leaders know how to cultivate this sense of teamwork.

If you want to go fast, go alone. If you want to go far, go together.
—AFRICAN PROVERB

Teams aren't a modern revelation. They were around a long time before the first business—or football—was launched. Our ancestors endured because they were tribal and their chances of survival were a whole lot better when they worked together. People in tribes knew what each member was supposed to do, and they trusted one another to do their jobs. The people responsible for getting the meat for dinner didn't worry about how they were going to find the vegetables, make the fire, or take care of the kids while they were out hunting. They trusted others in their tribe to do those things. That freed them up to spend the whole day doing what they did best, confident they would return to the cave and all those other tasks would be done. Those people are our very distant relatives, but we evolved from them and our brains are still wired like theirs. We're built to survive by working in teams. We have a natural inclination to work as a team, yet in business, leaders seldom create an environment that supports teamwork.

Most businesses survive and even thrive on the backs of a handful of people. As a business grows, the effort those few people have to put in doesn't decrease—it *increases*. Because instead of taking full advantage of *all* their resources, leaders figure out really quickly who they can rely on to get things done, and they tend to let everyone else sort of slide.

You can imagine what happens with those people who are doing the lion's share of the work. They get burned out. They lose their passion for the work and they quit. That leaves a gaping hole in the effort required to run a growing business.

If the top one-tenth of your people left, what would happen to your business?

It's like tug of war. If you have ten big, burly players on your team and the other team has a hundred smaller players, as long as those hundred players are doing their part and pulling on the rope, they'll wear out your ten guys eventually. But if you put another seventy or eighty players behind your rock-star rope pullers and get them to pull their weight, your team won't wear out. It will go further, faster, and it will endure.

You probably have people in your business who spark change. They can't carry the whole load, though. You need to involve everyone eventually, and that's where the team comes into play.

In your business, there are two main types of teams: those directly involved in making your products, providing services, and collecting the money, and those that support those teams.

The first set of teams typically comprises marketing, sales, engineering, manufacturing, delivery, customer service, and billing. Teams such as IT and human resources support these teams. Every team has a specific function and so when you're building teams, it's necessary to identify that function and populate the team with the right people, working toward fulfilling that function. Before all that happens, you have to create an environment where these teams can flourish.

If you want hundreds of thousands of people interested in your product, you need the entire marketing team working together to make that happen. Not just the social media people, not just the lead generation people, and not just the technology people. You need all of them working together. From there, the sales team takes over, with business development and sales and customer support. That's how the work gets done—teams make things happen.

Unfortunately, especially in Western culture, we celebrate the hero, not realizing the hero is standing on the shoulders of the team. And so we design our businesses for the individual—the hero—instead of for the team.

The shift from focusing on the individual to focusing on the team starts with you, the business leader. Getting the best version of every one of your individual human resources takes changing your mindset from one that believes it's okay to rely on (and typically, reward) a handful of people to one that looks to *all* its people. It takes recognizing that your business's success depends on creating an environment where teams thrive.

CREATE GREAT TEAMS

Great teams require people who believe what you believe—not just the most skilled people. You can train them for skill.

Often, we want to get the job done fast, so it's easy and convenient to hire people who can hit the ground running, with little to no training. If we then see that the person is a bad fit for the team, we ignore the problem, focusing on their immediate impact and figuring that they'll fit in eventually. We almost always regret those decisions because the odds of a person changing are slim.

You'll go further, faster and be able to sustain that

momentum by looking for people who are excited by your vision and eager to be a part of it. Teams thrive when the people in them share similar values and believe in a common purpose. Beyond that, they need some skills, but they don't need to be experts at the job—they can learn. I would rather hire the person with the minimum set of skills who's a great fit culturally over anyone who has all the skills and can start right away if there is a risk they are not a good fit for the company and team culture.

The more people you have working for you who share your values, purpose, and your vision for the company, the further and faster you will reach your goals. Instead of relying on a handful of people—your trusted circle— shoot for alignment with at least 50 percent of your team, with the goal of recruiting, vetting, and training a higher percentage of employees who also see your vision and are committed to helping make it a reality.

We'll get into more detail about hiring for teams in chapter 3, but once you have the right people, it's time to get to know them better.

GOOD NEWS, WEEKEND REPORTS, AND APPRECIATIONS

One of the best places to begin creating a team-building environment is in your weekly meeting.

Instead of jumping into your agenda, start by asking each of your people to share something about themselves with the group—preferably good news, but it doesn't have to be. In just a minute or two, each person gets to tell everyone one thing about their life at work or outside of work. Maybe they ran a marathon or their kid played a really good game of soccer. Maybe they took their family to a theme park, had a great first date, or wrote the first chapter of a novel. They could have started taking classes or bought a new car. On the other hand, maybe their car broke down on the freeway or a deer got into their garden and ate all their roses. Those kinds of Good News and Weekend Reports are okay too. Anything they want to share about themselves is great, as long as everyone gets a chance to speak. Be sure to share something about yourself too, but don't try to upstage everybody.

Then, at the end of the meeting, do what I call Appreciations. Each person on your team takes a moment to say why they appreciate another person at work. It could be someone in the room, someone on another team, or someone at a remote location. Maybe Bob stayed late one day to help them finish a report, or maybe Sally mentored them on a new application. If the person they're appreciating is in the room, then they get to hear it firsthand in front of their team members. But if the appreciation is for someone who isn't in the room, then immediately after the meeting, the "appreciator" goes to that person and tells them what they said in the meeting. If they're not at the same site, then the person can call them or send them an email. The important thing is that the person being appreciated knows that they're appreciated, and why.

Oh no, you're thinking, *meetings are already too long and we try to cram so much in! I don't have time for all this touchy-feely stuff!*

Good News, Weekend Reports, and Appreciations don't need to take a lot of time. If you have ten people on your team and each one can take thirty seconds for their share, that's five minutes tops! This is a great investment of time that will pay off in spades.

Also, you do not have to require that everyone participate every time. If you notice that one person abstains several weeks in a row, that may be a yellow flag and require com-passionate follow-up. Knowing you're reserving that time at the start and end of each meeting, people will hold them-selves and each other accountable for staying on track so they can each have a reserved space for individual talk time.

This is *not* the soft stuff; this *is* the hard stuff. Teams drive businesses, and healthy teams know and respect each other beyond the business. Seeing each other as human beings avoids or mitigates the lying, hiding, and faking that most people do at work to feel "safe."

If you make this part of your weekly ritual, you will learn fifty new things about your people every year. You will see your team in a different light and begin to understand them, their motivations, and their challenges. You'll see beyond their output and begin to see them as real people with full, complex lives just like yours.

Your people will show up with a different mindset. They won't dread the meeting—they'll be eager to show up and talk about themselves and the person they appreciate. When people are appreciated, they reciprocate by appreciating the people around them. They'll also get to know each other better and see each other as people instead of just coworkers.

A neurological side effect of starting and ending your meetings this way is that your people get a shot of dopamine, serotonin, endorphins, and oxytocin. These chemicals help to create a tighter bond between everyone in the room. Not only will each individual feel better about themselves, they will also feel better as a team. And after they leave the meeting, their behavior will carry over into their day-to-day work, where they'll be more likely to have each other's backs.

Start doing Good News, Weekend Reports, and Appreciations right away—today. Don't worry if they're not 100 percent smooth or if they go a little long the first few times. This is new for you and your team, and you will all get the hang of it soon enough. Over time, you'll experience higher levels of engagement, and when your team members see the results, they'll want to do Good News, Weekend Reports, and Appreciations with their own teams. There's a cascading effect that happens so that, in time, that healthy team dynamic spreads from you to your team, and to the whole company.

Expect people to be curious about your motives behind Good News, Weekend Reports, and Appreciations—even cynical, at first. If you haven't done this before, they might be trying to figure out your angle. You have to be totally sincere going into this with no ulterior motives other than getting to know your people and helping them develop a culture of safety and teamwork. This means that you, as the leader, have to go first and set an example of how to share this information.

Silicon Valley's celebrated CEO coach Bill Campbell was always about team. Eric Schmidt, the former CEO at Google, was one of Campbell's clients. In *Trillion Dollar Coach*, Schmidt talks about Campbell's influence on him and his leadership meetings at Google with Sergey Brin, Larry Page, and others. Before every senior leadership team meeting, Schmidt had everyone talk about their weekend. He did this purposefully to get people to share their lives with one another. Brin and Page were young at the time and always had exciting stories to share: kite surfing, mountain climbing, and whatever else young people in Silicon Valley do in their free time. Campbell and Schmidt wanted everyone to see their colleagues as human beings with lives outside of the office, and knowing more about each other brought them together and made them feel like more of a team.[11]

If you think this is just fluffy stuff that's not important and is going to take too much time from your agenda, try it anyway for a few weeks—just once a week, at the leadership meeting—and see how it goes. But if you're not the kind of person who can do that, then don't do it. You can't fake caring or sincerity, at least not in the long-term. If you just don't have it in you to care about getting to know your people and helping them feel safe at work, well, first off, I don't know how or why you became a leader at all, but it happens. So be honest with yourself—is this something you can do? If it isn't, or if you see it as simply a tactic to make your people more productive, then it won't work. You have to want this, not just for yourself or your company, but for your people.

This sets the stage for creating a team environment. By definition, a team is a group of people who share a common goal as well as the responsibilities and the

---

11   Eric Schmidt, Jonathan Rosenberg, and Alan Eagle, *Trillion Dollar Coach: The Leadership Playbook of Silicon Valley's Bill Campbell* (New York: Harper Business, 2019).

rewards for achieving it. A team readily sets aside individual or personal needs for the greater good of the group. A key benefit is that when people work for the betterment of the group and the overall organization, they are more productive, and will drive the business further, faster. These are concepts I've learned in books like *The Five Dysfunctions of a Team* by Pat Lencioni, have tested, and found to be true in my own work as a business coach.[12]

Good News, Weekend Reports, and Appreciations won't guarantee a great meeting, but doing them sets a positive tone for the people in the room. Instead of the typical chest-pounding and bragging that sneaks into meetings, everyone has a say, and that tends to humble everyone into keeping their egos in check. And it puts people in a more receptive mood for whatever happens next.

GET UP AND STRETCH: 3-1-1 EXERCISE

This exercise is for your leadership team. During your quarterly team meeting, give each person a few sticky notes—one for each person in the room, so if there are four people in the room, each person gets four notes. Then ask them to write the following on each note:

---

12   Patrick Lencioni, *The Five Dysfunctions of a Team: A Leadership Fable* (San Francisco: Jossey-Bass, 2002).

- Three things that each person in the room does that make the team stronger. (If there are four people on the team, each person writes nine positives total.)
- One thing that each person does that detracts from the team or makes it weaker. (If there are four people on the team, each person writes three negatives.)
- One thing that the author of the notes above feels he or she can do to be an even better team member. (Each team member writes just one note.)

Each person fills out one sticky note for every other person in the room: three things they do well and one thing they do not do well; then they write one for themselves.

Once everyone's finished writing, the leader of the group goes first, standing in front of one team member. That person reads their notes about the leader out loud, and the leader responds with "Thank you," and nothing else, as the team member hands the leader the sticky note. The leader then walks over to the next person and continues until everyone has read their note about the leader out loud, handed it to the leader, and received a "Thank you" for doing so. Then it's the next person's turn, standing in front of each team member, including the leader, hearing the positives and the negatives, saying "Thank you," and collecting their sticky notes.

Then, each person—beginning with the leader—commits to work on one of the sticky notes that year. It can be a negative that they work on, or a positive they will do more of, or it can be the one they wrote about themselves. It MUST be their choice to increase the chances of improved team performance. They also agree to receive guidance and accountability from the rest of the team to help them stay true to their commitment.

This is a difficult exercise for most people, but it's also eye-opening, especially when you do it regularly and you begin to see patterns in yourself and in others.

The only rules for this exercise are (1) the leader of the team has to go first and (2) no one can comment on the sticky notes they've been handed. They simply say "Thank you," and then commit to move forward, taking into account the feedback they've been given.

At each subsequent quarterly meeting, every person will provide an update on how they think they are doing on the item they chose. The team is to provide supportive feedback and their reactions to each person's updates. For instance, if the person thinks they have improved, but you experienced something different since the last update, provide the specific example and your reaction. I recommend saying something sincerely positive first, asking clarifying questions to ensure that you fully understand the person's path so far, and then describe the behavior or actions and your reaction. You must have the intention of helping the other person but also hold them accountable. Be kind, but honest.

KEY TAKEAWAY

Are you surrounded by the right people on your leadership team to achieve your vision? That is, do you have the *right* people in the *right* seats doing the *right* things *right*? If not, act immediately to train them up, move them over, or move them out. Your people are aware when these things *aren't* right and *they are waiting for you to act*. The business is suffering as a result—if it isn't now, it will be soon.

Running a company is hard enough with changes in technology, markets, and customers' needs. You can't control a lot of what happens around you, but you have a lot of control over who you hire and the environment you create. Instead of putting obstacles in your way, set yourself up to succeed with every action, every behavior, every hire, and every team.

This is a lot to ask, I know. There's already so much to do, but without making thoughtful, intentional decisions, your business will create its own environment—and it may not be the one you want. When you have a strong team, however, they will take you all the way to the championship.

Creating a team-building environment is only the first step to going further, faster. Once you have a rock-solid team in place, the next step is to create a culture where everyone feels safe to speak up.

GET UP AND STRETCH

Supporting information, exercises, worksheets, and bonus content are available at *Further, Faster Resources*: https://catalystgrowthadvisors.com/catalyst-growth-advisors/further-faster-resources/.

CHAPTER 2

CREATE A CULTURE OF PSYCHOLOGICAL SAFETY

When a flower doesn't bloom, you fix the environment in which it grows, not the flower.

—ALEXANDER DEN HEIJER

Simon Sinek speaks all over the world. The guy travels a lot, and he has a story which I'm paraphrasing here: Simon was staying at the Four Seasons in Las Vegas, and when he went to get his morning coffee, he asked the barista, "How do you like your job?"

The man said, without hesitation, "I love my job."

Simon then asked, "Well, tell me, why is that?" and the barista replied, "I come into work every day, and I work hard. Whenever a manager comes by, they support me. They say, 'What can I do to help you? What can I get you, and how can I support you in your role?' And not just my manager, but every manager. They are all there to make my life better."

The barista continued: "But it's a lot different at my other job. I also work at this other hotel, and when my manager comes by at that place, he's just looking for the problems. He looks for mistakes I made or tries to find anything that isn't just right. I keep my head down at that job and just collect my paycheck."

Simon asked the man, "What do you do at *that* job?"

"I'm a barista,'" he replied.

Same guy, same job, very different environment. He loves working at one place and he keeps his head down at the other. One is a psychologically safe environment and the other is not.

PSYCHOLOGICAL SAFETY

If stress kills people (or at least contributes to early death), and one of the top causes of stress is a person's job or workplace, then creating stress for your employees is literally killing them. Creating an environment where people feel unsafe and are pitted against each other, feeling like they have to lie, hide, and keep their heads down all the time is contributing to their demise. And no one leaves all that stress at work, either. We take it home with us and take it out on our families and other people we interact with. People spend one-third or more of their days at work—think about how what happens in that time affects the rest of their lives, including how well they sleep. There's a ripple effect, and as a leader, you have a lot of power and control over all those ripples.

According to Google's "Project Aristotle," where the company's People Analytics team sought to learn what made their teams most effective, researchers discovered "what really mattered was less about who is on the team, and more about how the team worked together."[13] From the report, in order of importance, they found the following qualities to be major contributors to a team's success:

1. Psychological safety
2. Dependability
3. Structure and clarity
4. Meaning
5. Impact

Along with the effect a psychologically unsafe environ-

---

13 Guide: Understand team effectiveness, *Re:Work*, https://rework.withgoogle.com/print/
    guides/5721312655835136/.

ment has on an employee, their family, friends, and coworkers, stress also affects the business. A person operating in an unsafe and stressful environment can't give you their best. They may have a wonderful idea for improving a product, service, or process; yet, how likely are they to tell anyone about it if they don't feel safe? "That's a stupid idea that will never work," versus "Tell me more about your idea—how will that work?" Think about all the innovative ideas your combined employee pool holds back if they're afraid of being ridiculed or ignored. Compare that with the effect they could have on your business if you were open to those ideas and could capitalize on them.

People should not have to believe their idea is perfect to try it out. You can encourage their innovation by reminding them, "We spent a lot of time interviewing you and choosing you among all the other candidates. We hired and trained you, and we believe in you. We trust that we made a good decision. So now we want to hear your ideas. We don't expect every one of them to be awesome or fully fleshed-out, but your insights draw on your unique experience and perspective, which we value. Here, everyone contributes their ideas—we don't act on all of them, but we're a better team and company when we consider them. So let's hear what you've got."

That attitude changes everything for your employees, and

instead of relying on 10 percent of your people for ideas, you've got another 90 percent coming up with ideas that other 10 percent never thought of. Think about how having ten times the number of people coming up with ideas could make your business more efficient, more effective, and higher performing. How might that change the morale in your company? How might that change your business and its ability to change the industry and the world?

Look around at the people who never offer up their ideas. They're not stupid—more likely, they don't feel valued, like they don't line up with the "superstars" in the company. They exist on the fringes, basically in fight-or-flight mode. They don't want to say or do anything "stupid" to draw attention to themselves or to get fired. These people do not feel like part of a team, and without their buy-in, there is no team.

You get their buy-in with a psychologically safe environment.

LEADING THE WAY

The first step in creating this culture is by showing people that you, the team leader, exist in a psychologically safe environment.

That means you're willing to admit that you don't know

everything. Ask people for their opinions on everything that you're making assumptions about. When you make a mistake, tell people about it. Show them your human side, and if you mess up and act badly—lose your temper or dismiss someone's opinion, for example—own up to it and apologize. Tell people you're aware of your shortcomings and are working on them, but in the meantime, the business keeps running and the world doesn't come to an end.

Start doing this intentionally. Practice it. And when other people make mistakes, act accordingly—not by vilifying them, but by accepting them for their mistakes and their willingness to speak openly about them. Instead of saying, "Oh crap, you really goofed that up!" you can say, "You did make a mistake, but we hired you because you're a great fit for our culture and very good at what you do. I know you have good intentions, so let's figure out how to make sure this doesn't happen again. How can I help you with that?"

Again, be intentional about this. Yeah, you're busy, and you think you don't have time for this. But in reality, you don't have time *not* to do it, because unless you're fostering this environment, your people will never feel safe enough to be their best for you.

Are there exceptions? Sure. If a person is doing something that violates your company's core values, or doing something illegal, that's different and should be managed accordingly. Typically, though, most mistakes aren't caused by a bad person or bad intentions. They are actual mistakes—errors in knowledge, in judgment, in execution. You owe it to your people and to your business to support them through the successes and the setbacks and remind them that you will not hang them out to dry because you're all in this together. A team.

Model this behavior and your own team will notice and begin to feel safe enough to imitate it. Then their teams will do the same.

When Toyota rolled out its Total Quality Management program, they encouraged everyone and anyone to stop production if they saw a problem—*any* problem. At first, people were hesitant to act. What if they stopped the production line and there wasn't really an issue? What if they caused the company to miss a deadline? What would happen? In time, they learned it was better to risk a mistake by pulling the chain than to ignore an issue and potentially push a hundred cars through the line that had problems. And when they stopped the line and didn't get in trouble for it, they began to feel safe. As a result, their quality improved. Eventually, other manufacturers that were pushing products through assembly wanted to replicate Toyota's success.

But the workers didn't institute this on their own. Leadership at Toyota set it up and had to stand by their decision to provide a psychologically safe environment for their people.

Your people need to know that as the head of the company, you lead the culture and set the stage for psychological safety. You might say something like this:

"Being psychologically safe is an underpinning of our culture. It's what we strive for, and it's on all of us, but it starts with me. I want you to look forward to coming to work every day, knowing this is a great place to work and a safe place to be. If you don't feel that way, I have work to do."

GET UP AND STRETCH: BE THE TEAM MEMBER YOU WANT TO SEE IN THE COMPANY

To promote a psychologically safe environment in your business, start with this exercise for yourself and your leadership team.

Vulnerability Exercise: Think about something you did that you don't feel good about but have never addressed with your team. This could be a mistake you made or something you accomplished but felt your performance was subpar. In your leadership meeting, admit this to your team. Describe what you did, why you're not happy about it, and what you're going to do to make sure it doesn't happen again.

It might go like this:

"You know that client meeting I attended last week at the trade show? I wasn't properly prepared. Even though we had Sales there and they did a great job, I think I could have helped them push it over the line if I had done my homework ahead of time, and I take partial responsibility for us not landing the deal. I know those guys and should have helped make it happen, and I think some people were counting on me to do that. I won't let that happen again, and here's what I'm going to do to make sure it doesn't."

This quickly shows your team that you know you're not perfect, you can admit your mistakes, and you're taking steps to be better. And that this behavior isn't only acceptable, it's necessary for you all to grow individually, as a team, and as a company.

TRUST

For people to feel safe, there must be trust among all members of the team. By trust, I don't mean blind confidence, but instead, the trust that comes with knowing other team members have your back and are open to hearing your ideas.

Trust arrives on foot and leaves in a Ferrari.

—MARK CARNEY

"An Integrative Model of Organizational Trust" defines trust as a "willingness to take risks," and further, provides the three perspectives of trust as *ability*, *integrity*, and *benevolence*. Here, we are focused on benevolence, "The perception of a positive orientation of the trustee toward the trustor."[14]

For example, *This person or company is much less likely to lie to me as I believe they have my best interests in mind.* Trust is also about showing vulnerability: that I am also a flawed human being who does not know all the answers, thus showing benevolence due to our shared humanity and imperfection.

In *The Five Dysfunctions of a Team*, Patrick Lencioni states that "The first dysfunction of a team is an inability to trust one another." The author believes that this inability to trust forms the foundation for the other four dysfunctions: fear of conflict, lack of commitment, avoidance of accountability, and inattention to results.[15] To avoid these dysfunctions, you have to have trust.

---

14 Roger C. Mayer, James H. Davis, and F. David Schoorman, "An Integrative Model of Organizational Trust," *The Academy of Management Review* Vol. 20, No. 3 (July 1995), pp. 709-734 https://www.jstor.org/stable/258792.

15 Patrick Lencioni, *The Five Dysfunctions of a Team: A Leadership Fable*, (San Francisco: Jossey-Bass, 2002).

Looking at it a different way, imagine how having trust affects teams in a positive way. With trust, conflict can thrive in a healthy way. You need this to happen. Without it, everyone's agreeing with everyone else. Disagreement and healthy conflict are how ideas are discussed and evaluated and how decisions are made. With that healthy conflict, people feel like they've been heard, and they're open to committing to whatever decision is made, even if it isn't theirs. Once a person is committed to a decision, they'll be more likely to hold themselves accountable for holding up their end of it, and ultimately, they will pay attention to the results.

GRAY MATTERS: THE SCARF MODEL

The NeuroLeadership Institute, an organization that studies how the brain and leadership work together, refers to the SCARF Model that was developed by neuroscience leadership expert Dr. David Rock to describe how our brains continuously move us toward rewards and away from threats. The acronym stands for Status, Certainty, Autonomy, Relatedness, and Fairness.

The problem is that our brains do not distinguish between physical threats and social threats. The same parts of the brain that light up when a person is threatened with physical harm also light up when that person feels threatened because someone embarrassed them, scolded them, or did something else that threatened their social self. To combat those threats, our brains work to help keep us safe. The brain can confuse a social threat for a physical one. Adrenaline begins to flow, other parts of our brain begin to shut down, and blood may be pumped into our muscles; we may begin to sweat. This is your brain preparing you to fight, flight, or freeze in order to survive.

If your boss came to your desk and said, "Come to my office right now—I need to talk to you," you perceive her words as a social threat because they challenge your certainty. You don't know what she wants to talk to you about. Her command also threatens your status because now you have to march on over to her office—her turf—where she definitely outranks you and has the upper hand. Your relatedness is also in jeopardy because you're being singled out and separated from the social safety of your team. If you think too hard about it, your sense of fairness is also lighting up as you wonder if whatever she wants to talk to you about will be a fair conversation with a fair outcome. At this point, you're barely out of your chair and already in full threat mode.

The walk to her office is a blur because you're making your legs move, but your brain is yelling at you to run the other way. You sit down and stare at your boss across the desk. She's saying something, but what? You can't listen, and you're not going to remember any of this because your brain is telling you that injury and possibly even death are imminent. Why are you just sitting there?!

This is what our brains do to us. Most people don't know this is happening or why, when the fact is, these responses to threats are what kept our ancestors alive and keep us alive, too, as far as physical threats are concerned. But for social threats? Not so much.

As a leader, consider the SCARF Model when you approach people. Instead of telling them to meet you in your office (and watching their eyes fill with terror), say, "Hey, you did some really great work on this latest project. I would like to get your perspective on what went well and how we can take our learnings from this project to help improve future projects. When you have some time, I'd like to walk through this with you. Can we grab lunch later this week?"

Think about how talking to the person that way changes the whole dynamic. Now, you're asking to meet in a neutral environment, removing the status threat. You've told the person what you want to talk to him about (certainty), and the challenges to his autonomy, relatedness, and fairness have been greatly diminished or removed. This is a very simple example of setting up a psychologically safe environment for someone.

INTENTIONAL TEAM SAFETY

Amy Edmonson has been studying teams for decades and written entire books about them. She says that people are at their best when they're feeling safe. They can screw up, admit a mistake, or say they don't know something and not have to worry about others thinking less of them. That's the environment you want to create for your people. Without it, they won't tell you the truth.

No one does this intentionally. We just get busy—busy with working on the business and forgetting why we started it in the first place. But all the other work you do, in and on the business, will never be as effective as it could be if your people don't feel psychologically safe working together in healthy teams.

This is why those "gut checks" are necessary. You think you know what your customers want, but unless you ask them about the struggles they're having, you won't know for sure. Likewise, improving the culture at work means actually talking to your employees. Instead of assuming you know what they want and need, ask them, "What are the most important things in your life?" and "How can I make your life better?" and "What are you struggling with personally, professionally?"

KEY TAKEAWAY

Get comfortable with "I don't know," "I need help," and "I'm sorry." Companies that go further, faster are fueled by trust. When you dare to be vulnerable, to show that you are human and imperfect, the team will respond.

They will stop lying, hiding, and faking. They will take more risks and challenge you more often, and velocity will increase. Be human.

Game-changing ideas can come from anywhere in your organization. The odds of them filtering up to you increase considerably when you hire the right people and let them know they can talk freely about their ideas without fear of judgment or ridicule.

Once your team trusts the people around them and feels safe in the environment you've created, it's time to make sure people are engaged and productive so that your company exudes excellence.

GET UP AND STRETCH

Supporting information, exercises, worksheets, and bonus content are available at *Further, Faster Resources*: https://catalystgrowthadvisors.com/catalyst-growth-advisors/further-faster-resources/.

CHAPTER 3

—————

PRODUCTIVITY AND A VISION OF EXCELLENCE

To the person who does not know where he wants to go, there is no favorable wind.

—LUCIUS ANNAEUS SENECA

Kip Tindell, the guy who started The Container Store, didn't create a business with the sole purpose of making money. He wanted a place where people could help other people sort and organize their stuff. A place that helped them make their lives easier. He wanted to make a place that people wanted to come to because they enjoyed being there—team members and customers alike.

Sure, it's a retail store but talk to anyone who's been

to The Container Store. More often than not, they go there with an idea of what they want and come out with something else. They usually end up spending more too, because the store clerks are part of that vision of helping people solve their problems. They don't just help people find what they're looking for—they talk to them, ask them questions, and try to understand the problem. Then they use their extensive training to help them solve it.

This is the business Tindell created by design. He didn't tell his people, "Get as much money as you can out of these customers." He said something more along the lines of, "Figure out the problem they're trying to solve and then use your knowledge of containers to help them find the perfect solution."

So if you go into one of these stores and say, "I want a box," the clerk isn't going to guide you to the shelf of boxes. They will ask what you want to do with the box. What's the box's job, what problem is it going to solve, and how would you describe the ideal outcome you hope to get from this box? They try to understand the essence of the problem instead of going straight to the product that you assume you need.

The Container Store people are trained to do this. And they love it. Every day they get to actually help people become more organized and make their lives better, and they get to do it better than the customer thought possible.

These employees go above and beyond too. They exceed expectations. One story tells of an employee who not only helped a customer find the perfect system for organizing all his tools, but he helped the guy install it in the parking lot. Who does that?

An excellent, engaged employee—that's who.

PUT YOUR PEOPLE FIRST

Too often, leaders skip over their people as opposed to putting them first. Many businesses still rely on the adage of putting the customer first, which by default puts everyone else—including employees—second, at best. The people who show up day after day rank lower than the ephemeral customers who come and go.

By now, you should understand that great leaders serve their people and not the other way around. If you take care of your employees, they will take care of your company and your customers.

No matter how high up the corporate ladder you go, never forget that you didn't get there on your own. CEOs and other leaders who think their title makes the company or the job all about them would do well to remind themselves of this fact. I recommend putting a reminder on your calendar every day asking, "What have I done *today* to make the lives of the people that work here better?" Because as leaders, improving the lives of our people is our responsibility.

So how can you improve the lives of your employees? Your first instinct may be to pay them more.

Data from a Gallup World Poll that surveyed more than 1.7 million people determined that those earning between $60,000 and $75,000 a year had optimal emotional well-being, which aligns with past research on the topic that found people are happiest when they make about $75,000 a year.[16] The return on happiness diminishes as the salary goes above that amount.

Yet leaders still ask themselves, "I pay my people so much. Why can't they just do what I need them to do?" Well, it's not all about the money. Sure, you don't want your people living paycheck to paycheck, or coming to work worried about how they're going to pay their bills. But throwing more money at them isn't the solution to employee engagement or productivity.

---

16   Jamie Ducharme, "This Is the Amount of Money You Need to Be Happy, According to Research," *Money*, February 14, 2018, http://money.com/money/5157625/ideal-income-study/.

GRAY MATTERS: ENGAGEMENT

From the neuroscience point of view, when a person is most engaged, two contradictory needs are at work: the need to belong and the need to be unique. When the satisfaction of these two needs intersects, the person feels engaged—which seems to make no sense. It's counterintuitive.

If you don't believe me, think about punk rock, tattoos, and iPhones. Every person who's into these things celebrates their uniqueness by doing pretty much exactly what a lot of other people are doing. The slogan "Think Different" was the subject of a humorous meme years ago, displayed over a photo of rows and rows of people all using Apple Macs.

Creating an environment where people can fit in while at the same time remaining unique is the secret to attracting the people you want—people who will be totally engaged in the company and what they can help you accomplish. At the same time, you repel people who don't align with your beliefs and won't get behind your purpose.

YOUR VIVID VISION

A better way to get more productivity and employee engagement is by sharing your vivid vision (see Cameron Herold's book of the same name for more information—this and dozens of other book recommendations can be found on my website; see Appendix for details) with people and inviting them to be a part of it. Your vivid vision is, in a nutshell, the reason you started the business and where you see it going. It's an imagined view of the business you want to build.

People want to be part of something bigger than themselves. We all want to belong, while at the same time stand out. The crossing of uniqueness and belonging is where we are at our best.

What are you trying to accomplish, and what does that look like? It's built on your core purpose and similar to a mission statement but much more personal. You have to mean it. Your vivid vision can't be just writing on a wall or web page. It's supported by your core values, which are the rules you and your people live and work by. Think about the behaviors you want to see in your people—and not just when they're in the spotlight, but when no one's looking. Your core values are "how we behave."

Your core purpose keeps you grounded. While you want the business to grow, you also want to make sure that growth doesn't violate your identity. Take CVS, for example, whose core purpose is helping people on their path to better health. Yet, until 2014, the company sold cigarettes. That year, they removed cigarettes from their shelves, because even though it was a profitable item for them, encouraging people to smoke didn't fit with who CVS is. It's not in line with their core purpose. Initially, the company took a hit, but within eighteen months, their earnings per share rose considerably. They knew their core purpose and made an intentional decision to stick to it, which paid off in the long run.

Setting all of this in motion—putting people first, showing them who you are, why you're there, and what you intend to do together—gives them a vision they can get on board with and be a part of, instead of sitting on the sidelines, not knowing why they do what they do or the big picture impact it will have.

Sharing your vivid vision with people lets them know that you trust them with your most intimate feelings about the business and your vision for its future. You're saying, "This is where I started and this is where we're going. I'm giving you all this great information that's been in my head because I trust you. You could take it to a competitor, but I trust you and I value you and what you have to offer to help make this vision a reality. I need you to want to do this too, though, for us to work together, but if you don't, that's alright too."

This act of sharing, of inviting people into your vision, helps to create the relationships you need for your people to be better, happier employees and better team members. People want to know that you trust them and are interested in them, and interested in what they can bring to the table.

So share your vision, explain why it matters to you, and show them how they can provide their unique talent to help the company realize that vision. If they buy into it and want to provide their skills and expertise, they should want to work with you. If that vision doesn't spark something in them, though, then they won't be happy at the company because they will be surrounded by it every day. If that's the case, accept it and let them know it's okay to opt out. Remember, this is still a safe environment and no one has to buy into everything you're selling if they're not feeling it. You can even offer to help them find their next job if you like, and write a letter of recommendation for them.

Train yourself to ask people how they're doing. Learn people's names and find out what they like about their jobs. And if you need some kind of therapy to get there, get it. Even though you've probably been going through life—like many of us do—pretending you're good at everything and don't need any help, you might need help with people. That's nothing to be ashamed of. In the meantime, make sure you have someone else on your leadership team who is comfortable being that role model for everyone else. Put them in charge of communicating your vivid vision, inviting people to be a part of it, and gauging their interest.

You have to ask questions and be interested. You have to admit when you don't know the answer. You have to believe in yourself but understand that it is impossible for you to know every answer. And you have to trust others enough to be vulnerable. If you don't, no one else will.

DESTINATION AND PURPOSE

Research about what people want from their leaders regularly shows that people want two things from you: (1) They want to know that whatever you tell them is true; and (2) Where are we going, and how can they help? People want a destination and a purpose. They want to know where the business is going and why. Purpose keeps us moving toward a destination, illustrated ultimately, by the vivid vision.

Destination and purpose help leaders make decisions: being true to a purpose beyond profit and a clear understanding of where they are taking the business.

You've no doubt heard some of these more famous destinations:

- Bill Gates's vision for Microsoft of putting "a computer on every desk and in every home."

- Red Balloon's goal of "2,000,000 gifting experiences in ten to twenty-five years."
- Boeing's pledge to "Become the dominant player in commercial aircraft and bring the world into the jet age."
- And John F. Kennedy's promise to America: "We will send a man to the moon and return him safely to earth before the end of the decade."

Circumstances push people to settle. Many just end up working for a paycheck, with no real passion for the work. No purpose. Given a choice, though, people want to be part of something bigger than themselves. They want to get behind something they believe in that they can contribute to and make a real difference.

If you give people a chance to provide value to that bigger thing, they'll give their blood, sweat, and tears to it. The ultimate metaphor here is the United States. People came to this country to be a part of something they believed in, and many made the ultimate sacrifice to get here and defend what they helped build.

If you're leading a company, and especially if you're the founder, you started with a cause, right? You believed in something bigger than yourself enough to get behind it and give it your all. It wasn't just about the money. You wanted to solve a problem, ease a pain, right a wrong. Think about how hard you worked to make that happen.

Don't keep that bigger thing all to yourself. Invite your people in and let them be a part of it too.

BEST OF WE AND BEST OF ME

We've all heard that most people at work are disengaged and that some are even actively disengaged and actually working against the company. The stats are startling and disturbing. Why do so many people disengage? And what can be done about it?

Business consultant, author, and Head of ADPRI People and Performance Marcus Buckingham wanted to know why some companies are more productive and have better cultures than others. After a lot of research, he discovered eight statements people make that describe what he called the "Best of We and Best of Me." These statements told him how engaged people were:

1. I am really enthusiastic about the mission of my company.
2. At work, I clearly understand what is expected of me.
3. In my team, I am surrounded by people who share my values.

4. I have the chance to use my strengths every day at work.
5. My teammates have my back.
6. I know I will be recognized for excellent work.
7. I have great confidence in my company's future.
8. In my work, I am always challenged to grow.

Statements one, three, five, and seven refer to the "Best of We," or how a person feels about the company, while two, four, six, and eight refer to the "Best of Me," or how they feel about themselves at work. Consistently, the results of Buckingham's surveys showed that employees at the best companies shared these sentiments.[17]

GET UP AND STRETCH: BEST OF WE AND BEST OF ME

To help you find out how closely your people align with the Best of We and Best of Me statements, I created an example survey. Feel free to create one like it for your people. You can find it here: https://catalystgrowthadvisors.com/catalyst-growth-advisors/further-faster-resources/.

Setting up the survey so the answers are anonymous will likely lead to more candid responses. If your company has a healthy

---

17 Marcus Buckingham and Ashley Goodall, *Nine Lies About Work: A Freethinking Leader's Guide to the Real World* (Boston: Harvard Business Review Press, 2019).

culture already, and people are used to speaking openly and honestly without fear of repercussions, you may want to have them use their names. That's your decision to make.

If you offer the survey anonymously, you can get further details by asking those who gave low scores a chance to go into more detail if they feel safe doing so. You can also set up regular lunches with the team. No predetermined agenda—just a chance to let them hear your plans and an opportunity for you to hear from them.

This survey will give you a baseline and show you how engaged your people are—or are not.

You might be surprised by the results of the survey. They might actually be alarming. They usually are (I'm not kidding). But no matter how negative they are, don't feel like you have to give up the ship or think it's a lost cause. You have it within your power to make major improvements to your company's culture. But you can't do anything if you don't acknowledge the current state it's in.

This isn't a problem that will go away on its own, and as your company grows, it will only get worse. Going further, faster means looking your issues square in the face and doing something about them so you can keep going while reducing the risk of falling flat on your face. As your business grows, you're pulled in more directions and will have less time and mental capacity to spend on things like culture, so get it sorted out now and then keep it healthy going forward. We'll talk about how you do that in the next couple of chapters.

How do you think you should handle it? What if, instead of getting all riled up and meeting with HR about how you're going to solve this culture problem, you meet with your people and tell them that you took the survey too? What if you tell them that you were surprised by some of their responses, but that you were also surprised by your own responses? Maybe you can tell them that the survey didn't solve anything, but it did shine a light on some issues that exist across the organization that are affecting all of you. But guess what? You are all human. You've all made mistakes—even you. You're also all in this together—a team—and together, you will figure out what to do about these issues.

GET UP AND STRETCH: PAY REGULAR AND SINCERE ATTENTION

People do better when they know someone is paying attention. Ignoring them has the opposite effect. The attention doesn't have to be lavish, but it should be frequent enough so they know you're thinking about them. Just checking in on everyone for a few minutes a week can make a difference. The attention can be as simple as asking them a few questions:

- What did you really enjoy about this week? What, when you were doing it, caused time to fly by for you? (Help them to do these things more often.)
- What's your highest priority this week?
- How can I help you achieve it?

I recommend the last two questions be asked *every week* during your Weekly 1:1s with your team. According to research reflected in *Nine Lies About Work*, that weekly touch is more effective than waiting to speak with people monthly or quarterly. In fact, talking to your people once a quarter is worse than not talking to them at all. They can see that it's just a formality and not sincere, and they feel unappreciated—like you really don't understand or value them and what they do. The research found that positive attention is thirty times more effective than negative attention (focused on what the team member does wrong) and *1,200 times* more effective than no attention in helping to create a high performing team.[18]

When you have these touches, don't use the time to tell people what to do or you'll encourage learned helplessness. Why should anyone figure out what to do or how to do it if the leader is going to tell them something else? Instead, ask them about themselves and their work. This tells them that you trust them to know what they're doing and to know if they need assistance.

---

18 Buckingham and Goodall, 2019.

KEY TAKEAWAY

Your team wants two key things from you: they want to know what you tell them is true and they want to know where the business is going. Write your vision down. Make it clear. Repeat it often. Don't stop until your people start finishing your sentences for you.

You have values. You have a purpose for starting and running your business. You have a destination and a vision. This is how you build a foundation for a successful business where people want to work, and where you take the business further, faster.

The next step is to continue this process with more actionable items. You have the right people, so now you have to figure out what everyone should do. Creating a function-organizational chart and a key process flow map gives your people structure and direction so they know what they're responsible for in the organization.

GET UP AND STRETCH

Supporting information, exercises, worksheets, and bonus content are available at *Further, Faster Resources*, https://catalystgrowthadvisors.com/catalyst-growth-advisors/further-faster-resources/, including the following:

- *Vivid Vision* **Book Link**
- **"Best of We, Best of Me" Employee Engagement Survey**

CHAPTER 4

ESTABLISH A FUNCTION-ORGANIZATIONAL VIEW

We squander our time dealing with exciting "crises" or attending pointless meetings. We fragment our time instead of consolidating it into large chunks during which we can escape the tyranny of the moment and think how the future might be radically better than the present.

—RICHARD KOCH, AUTHOR, *THE 80/20 MANAGER*

A multinational industrial corporation, which I'll refer to here as Acme Corp., brought me in to coach their leadership team. The company, which has been around for about a hundred years, employs a lot of engineers and is heavy on technology and manufacturing.

I met with each member of the leadership team individually and asked them to sketch out an organizational chart for me so I could see where they believe they fit. Usually when I do this exercise, I get pretty similar looking charts from everybody. With Acme, I got three: one with the current CEO as the head of the business; a second with the previous company owner as the head; and a third version that showed them as co-leaders. The versions were divided evenly between the nine leaders I spoke with—three, three, and three.

Clearly, Acme Corporation's leadership was not on the same page, figuratively or literally.

I took the three versions of the organizational chart to the CEO and said, "This is a problem."

Before we could go forward, we had to deal with this obvious misunderstanding at the highest levels.

GETTING ALIGNED

When I'm brought into a company to help them get further, faster, instead of meeting with the leadership team, I meet with every person on that team *individually*. I ask them questions. Interview them. This is how I get to know them and allow them to get to know me. It's how we start to build trust and rapport.

It's also how I get their unvarnished opinions about the company and their role in it. How is it going for them as a leader and as a member of the leadership team? What's that environment like? What are they supposed to be doing and how well are they doing it? I'm more likely to get candid responses without their peers in the room to influence their answers, and it's easy for them to talk to me because I'm still a relative stranger. I don't know their history with the company, and I have virtually no opinion of them. I'm this unbiased person who really wants to know their opinion on things.

I tell each person, "This conversation is going to be as confidential as you want it to be. Whatever you tell me will go into a summary I present to your CEO, but nothing you say is going to have your name on it unless you want me to include it. So you can be 100 percent anonymous if you want to be. But since you are a member of senior management, I need your thoughts and opinions on what we are all going to be discussing through this process."

The process is simple, but the outcomes can be surprising.

After a couple of meetings and phone calls with Acme Corp., three people were moved off the leadership team. I didn't expect that, but I wasn't exactly surprised, either. When I conduct initial discussions with the CEO of a business, I let her know that there's a good chance not all members of the leadership team will survive.

This is what happens when a business leader steps back from their business and takes a closer look at what's going on; it often takes bringing in a third party with an objective view of the situation. The process doesn't always lead to moving people to other positions or letting them go; more often than not, those who need to move or leave opt out on their own. They can see the writing on the wall and know it's time for a change.

But now everyone was on the same page. Only then could we create an accurate org chart—but not just any org chart: a function-organizational chart.

FUNCTION-ORGANIZATIONAL CHART

Most people think of an organizational chart as a collection of names and titles. They make assumptions about the responsibilities that go along with the titles. Instead of making an organizational chart, I create a function-organizational chart—and I define the function first.

I start the process with the leadership team by asking, "What are the *key* functions that drive this organization?" We list them on a whiteboard and when everyone's given their input, I ask, "Are these all the functions, or is there anything we're missing that involves working with customers, building products, hiring, training, or anything else you can think of that hasn't been mentioned?" What I'm looking for are the key functions, so we may end up with functions that aren't really top-level but fit under another function. We table those because we want to start with a concise list at the highest function level. I let the team know that we can revisit the list later to see if we missed anything, but we typically identify all or most of the key functions quickly.

Next, we assign names to each key function: the person who "owns" the function at the highest level. Ownership doesn't imply the person does the job, but simply that they are responsible for it being done, by themselves or someone on their team. The key function "marketing" is usually owned by the CMO, and the main responsibility within that function is to create raw leads and turn them into qualified leads. The CMO probably doesn't create social media posts, manage SEO, or write the company blog, but they're still ultimately responsible for those activities, and the people who do them usually report to the CMO.

Function–Organizational Chart

HEAD OF COMPANY	Susan
MARKETING	Bob Judy Trent
SALES	Mark Joe Judy John
DEV	Ben Andrew
FINANCE	Christy
TREASURY	Christy
CONTROLLER	Rob Christy
HR/LEARNING/PEOPLE	Betsy
CUSTOMER SUCCESS	Paul Joe
LEGAL	Brad
DEV OPS	Ben Andrew Paul Jill

Creating a Function-Organizational Chart is a Simple Yet Vital Task for Connecting People and Purpose

When you do this exercise, avoid asking the senior person in the room for their opinion first. If you ask the CEO a question, no matter what their response, most of the other people in the room will likely agree with it or pretend to agree with it. This accomplishes nothing. You have to get honest answers from everyone in the room for this to work.

Three issues commonly arise at this step: (1) the head of the company's name ends up in a lot of boxes; (2) many people's names are in a single box, so no one person takes ownership of the function; and (3) some of the boxes are empty because no one knows who owns them. This opens up a big discussion, as you can imagine. When you're getting more than one name in a box, ask why: "Why do you think Steve owns this?" You discover a lot about your business this way, like maybe everyone thinks Steve is in charge of something—except Steve. Or maybe one function is really two functions with two separate owners.

The outcome has to be that every function has one owner. They can agree to own that function for one week, one month, or one year, but they have to be willing to be the owner for that time period and be accountable for that function.

This might seem like basic stuff, but if you haven't gone through the process with your team, don't assume that everyone understands the functions of the business and the owners of those functions the same way. When I work with companies, I don't make any initial assumptions at all, because so often they are not as obvious as you might think.

These discussions don't always go smoothly, and the conversations can get heated. Once we've identified who owns each function, we talk about the different activities associated with that function and how they should be accomplished, and people will not always agree. It helps to have someone like a business coach in the room to facilitate these talks, because we can be neutral and help maintain a level of civility. My goal is to help the company get further, faster, without any biases toward individuals.

No matter how intense the conversation, or how many meetings it takes to get the functions and organizational charts worked out, the end result is a huge sense of relief. The tension of not knowing, and of assuming without any real certainty, dissipates. And for people whose roles were never really clear, that feeling of relief is even more pronounced. Can you imagine working in a business where people were mad at you for not doing your job when what they thought was your job was actually someone else's? That's what it's like to work without a clear function-organizational chart that everyone agrees with and understands.

GRAY MATTERS: DIFFERENT VIEWS

The function-organizational chart exercise is necessary because each person has their own view of the world, yet we assume that other people see things the same way we do. Until we tell everyone else, "This is how I see it," other people don't *know* how we see it.

The brain likes clarity. If your brain is not clear, it will make things up, so some type of closure is reached. However, as we have seen, its assumptions can sometimes be very wrong and possibly cause consternation within the organization.

We have to share how we see the business—and not just once but many times. It's like advertising, where the message needs to be repeated again and again. Eventually, everyone gets it.

Once you've created the org chart, you can't stick it in a drawer or post it on an internal company site and expect everyone to remember it. It has to be published and discussed—regularly. It should become part of the conversation. If someone has a question about any function, they should be able to look to that chart and know immediately who to go to.

THE KEY PROCESS FLOW MAP

The key process flow map shows where the money starts and where it ends. The goal is to identify each step and associated function along the path between the two.

When I do this with businesses, the initial investment—where the money starts—is in Marketing, which is responsible for generating leads. Then the money goes through Sales, and sometimes other functions, and it always ends in the Finance department. Typically, money travels through four to eight steps, and the path isn't always linear. The money may go from one function to two others, and those functions feed into a fourth.

With one particular business I coached, there were only four functions in the key process flow map. That was it. Despite all the different departments, teams, third-party vendors, and so on, the business rose and fell on the success of these functions. That new knowledge was a revelation for the leadership team. Suddenly, amid all the moving parts of the business, they had clarity. Now they could see the path to greater efficiency and greater productivity. It all revolved around these four functions, and each one had an owner.

To understand how this looks on paper, let's say the key process flow map starts in a box called Marketing. From there, we draw a line, which we call Qualified Leads, to a box labeled Sales, the second process. Now the line may go back and forth while Sales is trying to determine if the lead really is qualified or not, but eventually it takes the lead or it doesn't. Sales turns the Qualified Leads into Deals (yes, you would typically call this a "sale" but I'm using the word "Deal" here to differentiate *sales* from *Sales*). Now Sales sends that Deal to the third process, which may be Manufacturing or Service, or whatever function takes care of the Deals. From there, it goes to the fourth process, which may be Installation or Implementation. Finally, the customer pays, and the process begins again.

Simple, right? One paragraph, four processes. This is how many businesses operate, yet leaders tend to overthink and overcomplicate the process. By taking an hour, sometimes less, to create a process flow map, they would have a better idea of what was actually driving the business and needed the majority of their focus.

The function-organizational chart and key process flow map show you what's important, and they also show you who's accountable for each process. So when you want to hold someone accountable for something, you know you're holding them accountable for the right thing. If you're not happy with Marketing because they didn't post a blog this week, don't focus on the blog—pay attention to the leads. That's their job and what they're accountable for. Maybe they get more and better qualified leads by spending their time cold-calling or following up on event leads. Maybe they have a big white paper campaign that's delivering awesome leads. If that's the case, do you really want to jump on them for focusing their time where they're most likely to fulfill their obligation in the key process flow map? Or give them grief over a blog?

You might nail down the function-organizational chart and key process flow map in a couple of hours or creating it could take several months. When I work with a business, each time I visit them, we review the chart and the map. Anything that wasn't decided at the earlier meeting, we discuss. If they've made a decision, great; if not, I ask them how important it is to make a decision that day. Sometimes we have a conversation and other times we set a date to discuss it further. I always ask, "Is there anyone here who absolutely thinks this needs to be resolved in this room today?" If no one speaks up, we move on. But you have to ask that question, and you have to ask it in an environment where people aren't afraid to speak up. Don't move on thinking everyone's been heard or a problem has been resolved. Someone has to take the lead to ensure this is actually the case, or those things just fester and they will come up later, many times in ugly ways. I often reiterate a phrase I learned from Netflix's Reed Hastings: "To disagree silently is disloyal." Count to ten, and if no one speaks, move on.

If you're working with a large team, you can have each person create their own function-organizational chart and key process flow map, then have them split up into two or three groups and compare charts and maps among themselves, and come up with one for each group that satisfies everyone in the group. Then take that one chart and map from each group and share them with everyone in the room and decide how you can make just one chart and one map, combining those from each group.

The image *Key Process Flow Map* illustrates a high-level map, with the images that follow drilling down into the key process Marketing and, within Marketing, Demand Generation.

Key Process Flow Map - Example

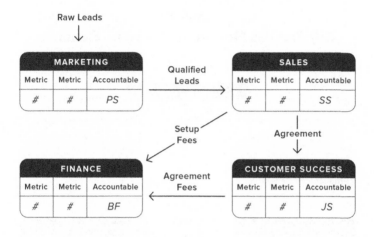

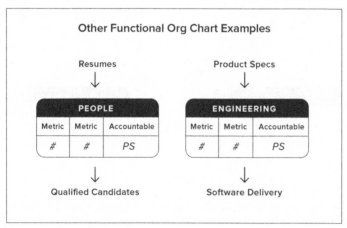

The Key Process Flow Map Illustrates How a Company Makes Money (Example)
Credit: Based on the Key Process Flow Map by Shannon Susko

One level down in the Key Process Flow Map, the image *Key Process Flow Map Phase II* illustrates four key processes of Marketing: Product Marketing, Product Management, Product Development, and Demand Generation.

ADVANCED

Key Process Flow Map PHASE II - Example

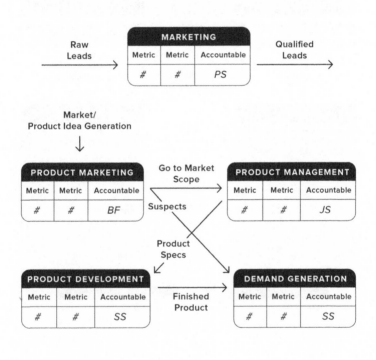

Key Process Flow Map II Shows Marketing and Its Processes as a Subset within the Key Process Flow Map (Example)

Next, the image *Key Process Flow Map Phase III* shows one of the key processes of Marketing—Demand Generation—and its four key processes: Awareness, Interest Generation, Qualification, and Sales Hand-Off.

Key Process Flow Map PHASE III - Example

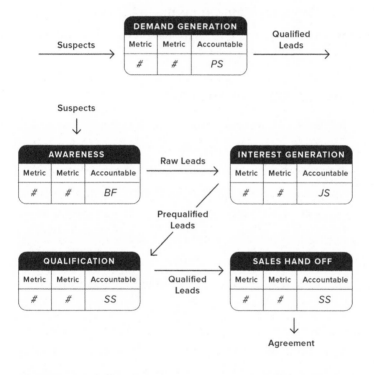

Key Process Flow Map III Details the Demand Generation Processes as a Subset of Marketing (Example)

In this example, the "Head of Company" (HOC) creates the high-level Key Process Flow Map, assigning an owner to each process. Then, the Head of Marketing creates their own Key Process Flow Map and assigns an owner to each process within Marketing. Whoever is assigned Demand Generation creates a Key Process Flow Map, which might include the processes shown here. Some businesses have three layers in their Key Process Flow Maps. Smaller organizations might be flatter, with just two levels, and large corporations could have many levels.

WHAT DO YOU LOVE—AND LOATHE?

The Head of Company can be the founder, president, CEO, or someone else. That person might be you. And if you're being truly honest with yourself, you're aware that you're doing more than one job. Besides Head of Company, you're also the Head of Marketing, Head of Sales, Head of Engineering...it varies. You might not have any of those titles, but you are functioning as such. As your company grows, trying to satisfy all those functions will lead to burnout.

You can't be the head of anything (and do it well) if you're burned out. Before you get to that point, you have to replace yourself in some of those functions. But which ones? Let's figure that out.

This is a super simple exercise that will help you decide

which functions to hang onto and which ones to give up. You'll have to find a replacement for those other functions, but let's not get ahead of ourselves. First, you need to identify your ideal functions—where you're going to actually work best in the company and avoid the burnout that's coming (if you're not feeling it already).

Get a piece of paper and draw a big letter *T* on it, as shown in the "Get Up and Stretch: Love It or Loathe It Exercise." At the top of the paper on one side of the T, write "I love this" and on the other side write "I loathe this." As you go through your workday, start listing things you love or loathe. If you worked on a task all morning and enjoyed it so much the time flew by and you can't wait to do it again next week, write that task in the "I love this" column. It could be a meeting, a report, anything. If you have this other task that you dreaded, put off, and eventually had to force yourself to do, put that in the "I loathe this" column.

You're going to have tasks that don't fit in either column and that's fine. Let's not worry about those. The goal here is to discover the extremes—those activities you spend your time on that get you pumped and the other ones that sap all your energy. Keep this paper handy, like in your top desk drawer, and make sure you write down everything you love or loathe.

Do this for at least a week—long enough to capture

everything you do. If there's something you do just once a month, quarter, or annually that you love or loathe, you can add those to your list too.

Now, look at your two lists.

In the loathe column, are you finding a lot of activities that fit under a particular function? Maybe you're going on sales calls and attending all the trade shows to meet new customers but you absolutely hate doing those things.

On the other hand, you look forward to the weekly marketing meeting where you listen to what's going on with that team. You enjoy guiding their approach, and you have a lot of creative ideas of your own to add to the conversation. Marketing loves your input.

You also really like those weekly calls with the research and development people. Your undergrad degree was in engineering, and you never lost your passion for technology. Those calls feed a need and they also help you fine-tune your marketing ideas.

Those lists should tell you something: it's time to fire yourself from sales. It doesn't play to your passions, and you're probably not nearly as good at it as you think. What if you had someone else who absolutely loves going on sales calls and talking to customers at trade shows take over those activities for you? This doesn't mean you have to skip the calls and shows completely, but maybe you could be more selective about the calls you go on and shows you attend. And maybe you can go to trade shows not to meet with customers, but for a different reason, say to get a feel for what other businesses are doing so you can bring that back to your marketing and engineering teams.

Follow the detailed instruction in the Love It or Loathe It Exercise, then fill in the worksheet or create your own lists on your laptop or on a piece of paper.

GET UP AND STRETCH: LOVE IT OR LOATHE IT EXERCISE

Writing down everything you love and loathe helps you understand the functions—and the tasks and activities within those functions—that you gravitate toward and should stick with, as well as those that you need to fire yourself from. This exercise, derived from Marcus Buckingham's "How to Do What You Love"[19] will show you what you need to hand off to others and where to focus your time. Follow the instructions below and enjoy all the extra time you get back every day.

---

19 Marcus Buckingham, "How to Do What You Love (in the Job that You Have)," *marcusbuckingham.com*, https://www.marcusbuckingham.com/rwtb/how-to-do-what-you-love/.

1. Throughout the week, as you go about your work, notice how you feel about your tasks and activities. If you especially love doing something, or it makes you feel strong, make a note of it under the "Love It" column. If you really dislike doing something or it makes you feel weak, drained, or bored, note that under the "Loathe It" column.

2. At the end of the week, look at your list. Thoughtfully pull out three statements from the "Love It" list that you are especially drawn to. These are likely statements that describe you at your very best. For example:

   a. "I loved coaching someone on the team."
   b. "I loved helping a coworker solve a difficult problem."

3. Move these statements from "love" language into "strengths" language. Knowing that you can't always coach a team member, you might write something like:

   a. "I feel strong when I help my team excel."
   b. "I feel strong when I troubleshoot difficult problems."
   c. "I feel strong when I create something unique and appeal-ing."

4. Think about how you might play to your strengths more in your role.

5. Develop a list of "weakness" areas as described above in a

similar way. Begin to think about how you might work around or through those weaknesses—remembering that we are biologically social and excel when we work with others as a team. Things to think about:

a. Can you delegate, automate, eliminate, or ignore any of these items?
b. Could you minimize the amount of time you spend in your areas of weakness?
c. Would anyone notice or care if you did not continue doing that item?
d. Perhaps someone who is strong in these areas could show you how to do these things more efficiently or effectively.
e. Or that person might be willing to take on some of these tasks if you are willing to help in areas where they are weak but you are strong.

LOVE IT OR LOATHE IT WORKSHEET

Love it (Strength)   Loathe It (Weakness)

1. _____   1. _____

2. _____   2. _____

3. _____   3. _____

4. _____   4. _____

5. _____   5. _____

6. _____   6. _____

7. _____   7. _____

8. _____   8. _____

9. _____   9. _____

10. _____   10. _____

The Love It or Loathe It Worksheet is also available at *Further, Faster Resources*: https://catalystgrowthadvisors.com/catalyst-growth-advisors/further-faster-resources/.

USE YOUR LOATHE IT LIST TO START FIRING YOURSELF FROM THE DAY TO DAY

The Love It or Loathe It Worksheet gives you a sense of what you gravitate toward, and it also works for the individual functions of a business. If you're the head of a company and you're not happy with some of your responsibilities, maybe someone else could do them. After you do this exercise, revisit it several times a year. As you progress, you should end up with a long Love list and an ever-shortening Loathe list.

Marcus Buckingham came up with the Love It or Loathe It exercise, and I've used it with a number of business clients. After you create these two lists, I recommend that you look at the Loathe column and leverage the method created by Rory Vaden, author and co-founder of Southwestern Consulting, by asking, "Is there anything on this list that I can automate?" Here's a great example: Do you set up meetings yourself? Research shows that it takes an average of eight communications to schedule a meeting. Instead, you could simply give people your calendar and tell them to pick an open spot when you're available (assuming you keep your calendar up to date, which you should).

Use a calendar app like Calendly to do this, or if you want to get fancy, try a software robot like x.ai's Amy that parses language, reads and writes, and makes it seem as if you're talking to an actual human assistant. That's one step.

The second step is to figure out which items on your list can be delegated. This is always a popular choice. Odds are, there is someone who actually loves those things you loathe and would love to take on those tasks for you.

Third, ask yourself if you can eliminate a task. We all do a lot of things out of habit, like writing reports. Are you writing reports, and if you are, is anyone even reading them? If this is the case, maybe you should stop writing those reports, or at least revisit them to see if there's any critical information that needs to be reported (maybe by someone else) that would eliminate the need for you to create an entire weekly report.

Finally, my personal favorite: procrastinate. Stop doing one of those things that you loathe and see if anyone notices. If they don't, maybe you can knock that one thing off your list. If they do notice, ask yourself whether you can automate or delegate the activity.

You may not be able to get rid of everything on your Loathe list, especially if you have a small business where people have to pitch in to get everything done. But if you find yourself with a ridiculous amount of work, figure out how much time it takes to get that work done every week. Be specific: How many hours and minutes a day do you spend on all these tasks? Now think about how much money your time is worth. One hundred dollars an hour? Two hundred? Three hundred? If you spend several hours a week on tasks you hate, you could be putting that thousand dollars a week of your time elsewhere, like growing your business and generating more revenue. Be conscious of how and where you spend your time, and use it for high-value activities. Hire someone else or outsource the work that *must* be done, but that you don't want to do, to someone else for less money.

Taking these actions is the first step in firing yourself from everything you do at work that you shouldn't do, so you can focus on what will get you further, faster.

FIRE YOURSELF FROM FUNCTIONS

Once you've completed your function-organizational chart, decide which functions or parts of functions you can and should fire yourself from. Just like with the Love It or Loathe It lists, consider where your top skills lie and what you truly enjoy.

Doing this exercise, you'll find that you've taken on roles by default and continued in them because you're the only person who can do them. If you started your own business, you were probably heavily involved in sales from the start because you had to make deals to keep the company afloat. But what if you hate sales? Do you have to continue heading up that function?

No, you don't. In fact, you might have someone in your company who's a better leader in that function than you, or it may make sense to hire someone new for the job.

When you're evaluating all the functions you're involved with, think about the individual activities associated with each one. Maybe you hate sales because you just don't like the lead generation part of it, but you love closing deals. If this is the case, you can stay on as the Head of Sales for now and bring in someone to head up business development. Once you get that person trained and running that function in the company, look at how you can hand off the other sales activities too, because eventually you should be running the business and nothing else.

You can do all these exercises on your own with no outside help, or you can assign the management and execution of them to someone in your company or bring in a third party to walk you through them. You know the dynamics of your business, so use your best judgment, but don't skip these steps. They're critical to getting your company and yourself to a place where you can move further, faster in your business.

Continue to work on firing yourself from anything that someone else could be doing. Focus on the big stuff. You'll find your sweet spot, and you may even come to realize that being the CEO isn't what's best for you or the company. It happens. Then you have a bigger decision to make, but it's not necessarily an awful thing. Plenty of CEOs have stepped down from the role to run other parts of their companies that they're more suited for or to spend time starting the next company.

KEY TAKEAWAY

Simplify your job and your business. Acme thought their business was much more complicated than it actually was, and the function-organizational chart and key process flow map proved otherwise.

Now that you have a high-level view of the business, understand the key inputs and outputs, and you know the kind of people you need to help you get the job done, it's time to build your teams. Let's talk about how you're going to hire people for those teams.

GET UP AND STRETCH

Supporting information, exercises, worksheets, and bonus content are available at *Further, Faster Resources*, https://catalystgrowthadvisors.com/catalyst-growth-advisors/further-faster-resources/, including the following:

- **Function-Organizational Chart Example**
- **Key Process Flow Map Example**

CHAPTER 5

///////////////

HIRE FOR TEAMS

...on the best teams, the team leader is able not only to identify the strengths of each person but also to tweak roles and responsibilities so that team members, individually, feel that their work calls upon them to exercise their strengths on a daily basis. When a team leader does this, everything else—recognition, sense of mission, clarity of expectations— works better.

—MARCUS BUCKINGHAM, *NINE LIES ABOUT WORK*

One of my clients was looking for a Doctor of Chiropractic Medicine (D.C.) to join his practice. Here is his first ad, which ran for about ten months:

> A Waiting List Practice in Natick, MA (MetroWest Boston) is looking for an ambitious D.C. with the right skill set to join our multi-D.C. growing practice. Applicant must be certified in Active Release Techniques®. Proficiency in

motion palpation and manipulation is desired. This is an excellent opportunity for the right D.C. to join a leading-edge, health and wellness-focused practice. We will train you for success! If you would like the opportunity to join XXXXXXXXXXX, please send your resume with a cover letter expressing your interest to: XXXXXXX

Over those ten months, my client received just one response and ruled out that candidate on the first phone conversation. Clearly frustrated, he rationalized that the reason he was not getting excellent candidates was the fact that Massachusetts was a more challenging state for new chiropractors due to licensing requirements, among other reasons. His frustration increased as, through our work together, we determined that hiring just one or two chiropractors could, more than any other action, enable him to triple the size of his business within just a few years—his BHAG.

We talked more deeply about what a great candidate would look like: the minimum skills they needed, what would make them a good fit with the staff and patients, and once they were up to speed, the expectations each party should have assuming a successful and achievable outcome. After this conversation, we crafted the following ad and he posted it on the same job board as the earlier one:

We are a successful practice in Natick, MA (MetroWest Boston) which operates with integrity and passion to help active people get out of pain, perform better, and live healthy lives. We are looking for an associate chiropractor that is certified in Active Release Techniques®, and proficient in Motion Palpation, and is interested in earning $200-300K (yearly) helping 35-55 patients daily to help us expand our practice. Interested doctors are invited to send a resume with cover letter to: XXXXXXXXX

My client had four responses in the first week. Within a short amount of time, he was able to hire a qualified candidate who was also a great fit for his business. Since then, he's also received inquiries from chiropractic students interested in working with him when they graduate.

By taking about thirty minutes to think deeply about the vital few aspects of the role from the company's and the candidate's perspective, we were able to describe exactly what a great candidate would find most attractive. The time saved in screening and interviewing mediocre candidates was far greater than the thirty minutes (ten months versus ten days) taken upfront to think not only what my client wanted but what the right candidate would value.

YOUR BARRIER TO GROWTH

I often ask leaders what their biggest barrier to growth is.

The most frequent response I get is how hard it is to find qualified candidates to help grow the business. I then ask them these questions:

- Are you hiring people who believe what you believe? That is, do you have a core purpose for the business and leverage it in the hiring process?
- Do you share most, if not all, the same core values? How do you interview with these in mind? Do you reinforce them daily?

If you want to grow your business and go further, faster, hire the right people who have at least the minimum skill level and knowledge to do the job. You can teach them the rest. However, you also should be growing the existing people in your organization by giving them a sense of purpose, continually put them in positions that take the fullest advantage of their strengths and passion, and provide them with a clear vision of the future.

Attract and hire people not only for what *you* want but for what *they* want too. Hire people who want to join your culture, not just do the job you're offering for a paycheck. Hire them into a position they can't wait to start and a team they cannot wait to be a part of, with the intention of allowing them to grow the role or into the role as a key part of the team.

Hire the right person for the team and the company. When you hire a person who's excited about joining a team where they're a good fit and working for a company they believe in, they'll be more productive, have a better attitude, and will be more likely to stay with you. They'll be an asset to the company—not as a quick fix to get the job done, but to contribute meaningfully to helping you and the team realize the company's vision.

While figuring out these "soft" things might seem like a waste of time, the effort can have tremendous bottom- and top-line results for the business. Ron Lovett, founder of Source Security & Investigations, found more than enough untapped resources hiding in plain sight. In his book *Outrageous Empowerment*[20], Lovett describes his journey and in a short video from the ScaleUp Summit Denver 2018,[21] he provides an example of trusting an existing employee that resulted in much higher levels of engagement. Worth thirteen minutes of your time!

Those people are out there or may already be hiding in plain sight within the company. If they are not, you have to find them, and you may have to change how you hire them. Typically, we hire people for a particular role

20   Ron Lovett, *Outrageous Empowerment: The Incredible Story Of Giving Employees Their Brains Back* (Charleston: Advantage, 2018).

21   ScaleUp Summit Denver 2018, *YouTube*, youtube.com/watch?v=eZ2fcJ-VETw&feature=youtu.be.

that requires a particular skill set. So when we're sorting through applications and resumes, trying to figure out who to interview, we focus on education and experience. Which candidates have the training and work history that will make it easy for us to plug them into the open req? It's not hard to understand why hiring managers do this: they are busy and it's an extremely efficient way to select the "right person for the job" from hundreds or even thousands of candidates. And it even works out in the short-term. The new hire knows the job and pretty much hits the ground running their first week.

That can be a linear and even myopic way to hire a person. You're hiring them for your short-term needs, instead of your—and their—long-term goals. How fulfilled is this person going to be when your company grows and you need them to stretch? How happy are you going to be when they tell you that's not the job they were hired for? Today's skills might not matter tomorrow, but the person you hire today should be the person prepared to take on today's and tomorrow's challenges to the greatest extent possible.

If you are reading this book, you want to grow your business. To do that, you have to grow your people to keep up with market changes, technology, competition, and customers' needs, among other things or they will be left behind. Hiring the best possible candidate who can grow with the company makes it so much easier down the road for you, them, and the business.

The other problem here is that hiring people for skills only means they may not click with other people on the team. What if they're highly skilled but so arrogant that no one wants to deal with them? Don't expect to learn this the first day, by the way, because everyone's on their best behavior that first day—and typically for the first three months. But by day ninety-one, you may discover that your quick and easy hire was a major mistake.

Any person you hire affects the whole team. If the team doesn't like a person, they'll avoid interacting with them. The team won't be as open to sharing around the person, even in meetings where you need people voicing their thoughts and opinions. This doesn't make your business go further, faster—it actually slows the business down.

Hire for a well-rounded team, not a well-rounded employee. Too often, we try to fix the weaknesses of the employee to fit into some arbitrary thing that we say is "the job." If we're hiring really good people whose core values align with ours and they're a good fit in every other way, we should find someone else to do what they cannot. People are different, and the likelihood of finding that perfect someone who checks all the boxes is slim. You won't turn an extrovert into an introvert or vice versa, and you won't teach someone to be creative who isn't. Take full advantage of what they're good at and strengthen those traits and skills to help them be even better.

Today, more companies hire people who fit the company's culture, and that's a step in the right direction. Even better is hiring people for the culture of the team they're going to be a part of. That team culture is likely an extension of the company culture, but it's still unique, influenced by each individual. People are more likely to stay in a company they don't like if they're a good fit for the team. Surrounded by people they get along with sort of insulates them from the rest of the business and the people in it. Likewise, they can love the company culture but if their own team's culture stinks, they're not going to be happy. They'll be less productive and will probably not hang around long either.

Hiring for skills is easy and that's one reason we do it. It's fast. It's simple. Tell us your skills, tell us what you've done before. Boom. You're a fit. Communicating the values, purpose, and culture of your business and getting people to demonstrate how they will support all that is a lot tougher. Most of us aren't good at that kind of interview because we haven't been trained to do it. How do you discover a person's values and personal traits that they'll bring into the company? Because you really are inviting a living, breathing human organism into your organization who's going to be interacting with all the other humans day in and day out, affecting their behaviors too.

Consider the typical interviewee—the candidate—if you will: they show you their best side. That person is always the ideal hire, because they won't show you who they really are until day ninety-one, when they're comfortable enough to let their guard down and be themselves. That may be the person you hired, but it may be someone entirely different too. They can do the job, but they're lacking important values like integrity, humility, and kindness. Or their behaviors are not what you expected—they're late for every meeting and never participate. Or they talk over everyone in the room. Letting someone go is difficult for more reasons than we have room for in this chapter, so let's suffice it to say that we should be avoiding that choice by hiring well to begin with.

FOCUS ON KEY INPUTS, OUTPUTS, AND TEAM

In my experience coaching leaders, I've seen the same mistakes being made again and again. Businesses don't attract the right kind of people. They hire primarily and sometimes solely for skills and not for fit. They want people who can hit the ground running, which is fine in the short-term, but won't hold up for the long haul. The people who are brought in aren't welcomed into the company, and the good people who stay aren't valued. These people aren't doing the jobs that they would like to do and may be much better at than the people who are currently doing them. This is where focusing on each person's strengths, weaknesses, and interests, and examining the roles within the business and how people's innate abilities might align with them, can get you further, faster.

Imagine if your people focused most of their time on what they do well and enjoy. How would that affect productivity? This is why you have to look at who you have already on your teams, make sure they are where they need to be, and then look for the roles that aren't being filled.

To get there, take a hard look at the key input and output of each role. Then look at your people. Are those who are struggling badly at their jobs, or are they in the wrong job to begin with? Is there another role where they'd be a perfect fit? Your people may not be even thinking about what they'd rather be doing because they're focused on their job description and nothing else. But if you make figuring this out part of the hiring process and instill it into an employee development process, you might be surprised by all the untapped talent you have within your ranks and already on the payroll.

USE YOUR 3X5 CARDS

Understand the kind of person you need to hire and how their results play to the role. For this, we can look to Dave Baney's *The 3x5 Coach*[22], which enlists one of the most basic office supplies for the task.

Three by five cards are simple yet tremendously useful tools when it comes to interviewing and hiring. You should have one for each function and subfunction, created when you made your function-organizational chart. Each of those cards describes the key outcome-based activities (no more than five) the owner of a function must perform in order for that function to be successfully executed. Each activity should have at least one key metric (and no more than three) to measure whether the activity is being performed well.

Work with your HR person or your Head of People, whatever you call that individual. Tell them the kind of person you need for the company and the team and ask them to devise a method for finding that type of person. They may have to do some research to discover the best assessments or techniques, and of course, they will need to be aware of what's politically correct and legally acceptable, but that's their specialty, so they should be able to handle that piece. Assessments like OCEAN (Openness,

---

22   Dave Baney, *The 3x5 Coach: A Practical Guide to Coaching Your Team for Greater Results and Happier People*, (Las Vegas: 55 Questions, 2017).

Conscientiousness, Extraversion, Agreeableness, and Neuroticism—the "Big Five Personality Traits") and HEXACO (which adds the "H Factor," Honesty-Humility, to Emotional Stability, Extraversion, Agreeableness, Conscientiousness, and Openness to Experience) and will help you figure out the kind of person you're getting.

Tell your human resources people that you don't expect them to nail it every time, but the closer they get to a good hire for the team, the happier and more productive you will all be, and the further and faster you will grow as a company.

This also makes it very easy for you to write a job description and to explain the job to a potential hire. That's what the chiropractor did earlier in this chapter: he changed his job posting from a skills-based description to a fit-based one. Write it so the candidate knows exactly what's expected of them, how they contribute to the team's success, and what defines success in the role. Make the conversation interactive. There may be activities the person loves to do and others they are capable of doing but don't relish. Have that discussion with the understanding that you don't expect them to love and excel at every task, but you want a clear understanding of their preferences so you can plan how they will fit within the team. This process, along with interviewing for values and assessing for personality, ensures that you've done your due diligence in the interview process and put your-self in the best possible position to hire someone who will be successful.

This image of a 3x5 card illustrates what a sample card might look like. The role Head of Company appears on one side of the card. On the back of the card are the outcome-based activities required to fulfill the function of the role. This example may be different than yours. Write what makes sense for your business. The only rules are that you cannot list more than five activities and they must be the highest value activities for the role.

Head of Company

Why do I get paid?

• Vision Realization	*60% + Gross Margin*
• "A" Players on Leadership Team	*100%*
• Brand Promise Delivery	
Net Promoter Score	*60+*
Repeat Customers	*95+%*
• Senior Leadership Development Plans	*100%*

3x5 Cards are Useful Tools for Ensuring You Have the Right Person in the Right Role. Credit: Derived from *The 3x5 Coach* by Dave Baney.

WELCOME PEOPLE TO YOUR BUSINESS

The last time someone left your company, you followed a process. There was an exit interview, and paperwork to fill out. Your IT people and HR people were busy taking care of their end of the departure, and the person's manager dealt with all the team stuff. Then someone threw that person a party. That's what we do when someone leaves.

Now, when you hired someone into the business, think about how that went. The interview process was intense, involving human resources, the hiring manager, and maybe the entire team. You may have even run a background check and a credit check, and you negotiated the terms—salary, commissions, bonuses, benefits—to get the best person at the best price. You put a lot of effort into that hire.

On day one of that person's life in your company, they show up and are led to their office or cubicle. There's a laptop, a company pen, and a company mug. Maybe a manual. The hiring manager is busy but someone on the team is going to show the person where the break-room, the bathrooms, and the coffee machine are. The IT person will come by later to show them how to login to their laptop. It's all haphazard, and that first day—often the whole week—is pretty awkward for that new hire. It's as if you courted this person so hard to get them to say yes, and now that you have them, you don't value them anymore.

If you're going to put all that energy into hiring the right person, welcome them the right way. Throw a party for them in the morning and do some icebreakers. Have the most senior person in the business—the CEO, if they're available—take them out to lunch. At three o'clock, when everyone's starting to wilt, have the hiring manager get them out of the building and go for a walk. Remind this person that you're thrilled they picked your company, and you're excited to see what they bring to the table. Don't wait for everything to go sour and then get to know them the day they walk out the door. Make your people feel wanted and welcome that first day, and every day, and they will want to be there.

RESCUE AGENCY ONBOARDING: AN EXAMPLE OF WELCOMING PEOPLE TO THE BUSINESS

Rescue Agency makes the first day great by filling it with meaningful experiences and interactions so the new team member goes home confirming the decision to join. Here is how they do it:

First Ten Minutes

The hiring manager is required to take the following steps well before the new team member starts her first day:

- **Show up early.** New hires often arrive early for their first day; do the same so that they're not waiting alone.

- **Don't wing it!** Have an office tour ready to go before they arrive.
- **Make introductions** during the tour. Encourage employees to invite new team members to come by their desks and say hello later on.
- **Deck out their desk** in swag, decorations, and a welcome card. End the office tour at their desk to keep the excitement going. Rescue Agency always has a welcome card hand-signed from team members as well as a welcome letter from the executive team.
- **Have their technology set up** and ready to go, with their email already pulled up on their screen. It's all smooth sailing from there!

Weekly Rescue Huddle

The hiring manager introduces the new team member and tells a few fun facts about them instead of making the nervous new employee talk about themselves before they are comfortable. For remote team members, the hiring manager sends out email introductions with a bio, a few interesting stories, and a short Q&A to help distributed team members find common hobbies and interests.

First Lunch

Whether they are at headquarters or remote, every new team member is invited out for lunch on their first day with their supervisor and direct team members. It's time for them to get to know each other, ask questions, and feel out relationships.

First Week

Each new team member is provided with a schedule of their first week, including meeting invites to social events. The main goal of the first week is designed to help the new team member get to know their team and socialize with the broader team to help them feel as comfortable as possible in the new environment.

New team members are also paired with an office buddy who is charged with integrating the new person into the company's social ecosystem.

First Six Months

Now that some time has passed and the new team member has acclimated to the organization and the role, it is time for both the team member and the hiring member to check in. Rescue continues onboarding activities beyond the initial onboarding for the role, operations, and culture. At the three-month mark, they check in with team members and essentially revisit every aspect of the initial onboarding.

Rescue Agency also uses the ninety-day milestone as an opportunity to check in with employees and begin to set goals for the future. By this point, new hires have had enough time to understand their roles and form meaningful goals, and it's a chance for both parties to address any concerns or lingering questions.

Ongoing Feedback Both Ways

Feedback to the new team member is important but also important are that person's impressions of all aspects of the organization. At some point in the first six months, Rescue Agency reverses the direction of traditional feedback and invites new hires to share thoughts on what they've learned, what they're still missing, and what you could do better. This is where creating that psychologically safe environment is critical, so the person is comfortable speaking up. Someone from HR also checks in weekly to give the new hire a chance to give updates along the way without having to schedule time themselves during a time where they may not be comfortable reaching out proactively to supervisors and others in the organization.[23]

23 Jillian Lukas Rodriguez, "4 Steps to a More Successful Onboarding Program," *Small Giants*, November 4, 2019, https://blog.smallgiants.org/employee-onboarding?utm_campaign=October.

GET UP AND STRETCH: CORE PURPOSE, OBJECTIVES, AND VALUES

Your core purpose and values for the business play a critical role in hiring team members, so if you haven't defined those yet, this is the time to do it.

Five Whys to Your Core Purpose

The essence of the Five Whys exercise is asking the question "Why?" enough times to get to the main truth—the deepest answer to the question, which you may not even realize until you do this exercise. In the Five Whys, your job is to find out why you started your business. What made you want to start your business? What was important about that reason? Keep asking why until you get to that nugget—the real why that inspired you to do what you do.

Howard Schultz tells a story of why he started Starbucks. He had a difficult childhood and wanted a place to escape to—not work, not home, but a third place he could go. Think Cheers or Central Perk. His why led him to build his own third place, which has become a favorite third place for millions.

Also, think back to the *When*. When you founded the company, what was going on in your life, and what impact were you hoping to make in the world? Your purpose may be found in the stories you tell.

Four Questions to Your Core Objectives

If your purpose is the why, your objectives are the what. Discovering your core objectives is possible by answering four questions:

1. What is our company trying to accomplish, and how will we accomplish it?

2. What are the objectives that matter most to our company?

3. Who matters most to the company? Who are the company's stakeholders? This includes employees, customers, shareholders, suppliers, and society at large.

4. What criteria have to be met in order for us to move forward with the decision?

Mission to Mars and Your Core Values

A popular core values exercise is Jim Collins' "Mission to Mars." Here, you discover the people who embody the essence of who you are as a company. These employees exhibit the behaviors that you look for in all of your people. When you identify these people, tell stories about them. The stories should reflect the values that represent the best of your business. They aren't descriptions of people, but actual stories about something the person did. Here's an example:

One of our core values is "professionalism." The way we describe this is, "When you visit a customer, you should behave as if you are a guest in their home."

Sally, one of our sales engineers, has a new client. She's going to have to spend a lot of time at their site over the next six months, helping them with a new installation. The week before her initial on-site visit, she asked her contact there if she could just come in for a short visit to observe the environment, talk to some people, see how they dressed. She had lunch with a couple of the IT people who'd be working with her on the installation and got a sense of how they interacted with each other. When she came in that first scheduled day, Sally was fully prepared to fit in really well. I want to call her out for taking the extra time to make sure that she was understanding what a guest would be like and how they would dress, talk, and behave as a guest at her new client's site.

Your company will have actual values and aspirational values. You need to separate the two and admit that your actual values are "Who we are," while your aspirational values are "Who we are becoming." If you don't do that, people won't believe you. If you say that your business represents integrity yet you have leadership that lies regularly and you haven't dealt with the problem, people will just roll their eyes, and you will be sacrificing your own integrity.

Once you've established your core values, you have to live them every day. Adopt the behaviors of these values as your own. Look for employees who adopt them and take that into consideration when you recognize, reward, and promote your people.

Resources for Core Purpose, Core Objectives, and Core Values are available at https://catalystgrowthadvisors.com/catalyst-growth-advisors/further-faster-resources/.

KEY TAKEAWAY

You, as Head of Company, have to be a change agent while creating the environment that welcomes other change agents and their ideas. Start that *now*, with your hiring process. Deep down, you already know there's a better way to hire people. You probably were never taught to do it differently, and your human resources people may be doing whatever they learned years ago. We all got into this habit of vetting candidates a certain way and that way may have been fine for jobs where people don't interact or work in teams, but for today's typical business, that process doesn't work anymore.

Some of the most successful companies in the world started hiring differently years ago, but their methods are just now catching on. Most companies still cling to the hiring methods that were passed down decades ago. New people may come in with new ideas, but the pressure to fit in can be overwhelming, especially for a new hire, so they go along to get along and nothing changes.

When your people are working in teams and you're bringing in more of the right people, and you've figured out all the key functions and activities that need to be accomplished to get further, faster, it's time to revisit your strategy. If you don't have a strategy, don't feel bad. Many leaders don't, or they think they do, but it's not really a strategy.

Part II is all about creating a strategy and a system for executing it. This section of the book can be completed in parallel with Part I, so if you are still working through this part, that's okay. Keep reading, and keep moving further, faster.

GET UP AND STRETCH

Supporting information, exercises, worksheets, and bonus content are available at *Further, Faster Resources*, https://catalystgrowthadvisors.com/catalyst-growth-advisors/further-faster-resources/, including the following:

- **Core Values Exercise**
- **Core Values Reality Check**
- **Core Values Sample Interview Questions Guide**
- **Core Purpose Exercise**
- **Core Purpose Reality Check**

CREATE A STRATEGY-EXECUTION RHYTHM (INTELLIGENCE SYSTEM)

CHAPTER 6

ESTABLISH DIRECTION

Perfection is achieved, not when there is nothing more to add,
but when there is nothing left to take away.

—ANTOINE DE SAINT-EXUPÉRY

Southwest Airlines is a company that understands strategy. They've been profitable every quarter for more than forty years, and their strategy is so simple, it can be summed up in two words: Wheels Up. When they have planes in the air, they're making money. Everything they do follows the simple strategy of getting more planes in the air every day than anybody else. When Southwest leadership has to make a decision, they only have to answer one question: Does doing it this way put more planes in the air or risk putting fewer planes in the air?

They look at everything through that lens, down to what goes on their menu. Southwest once considered serving chicken walnut salad to passengers because someone thought it would be a good idea. Customers wanted healthier, more nutritional choices. Yet, serving chicken walnut salads would *not* put more planes in the air. The ingredients would have to be delivered by refrigerated truck, and if the truck was late or the refrigerator broke down, the plane would have to wait, which meant fewer planes in the air. That's why you don't get chicken walnut salads on Southwest—you get bags of pretzels.

Southwest has used the same strategy since they've been in business. It's why they don't operate from a hub and do short-haul flights. They have a simple strategy that everyone understands, and they all follow it.

BE LIKE SOUTHWEST—HAVE A STRATEGY

CEOs want to know how to grow their business. When they reach out to me to help them do that, I often hear that they are not consistently hitting their sales goals. They believe they have operational and/or personnel problems that impact their ability to hit their goals. When I ask them what they're executing on, they don't know how to answer, because leaders seldom view their operations this way. So I help them out: "You're executing on a strategy, right? You've established a strategy and the activities you execute support that strategy; is that right?" They almost always agree. Then I ask, "If I asked each person on your leadership team to write down on a piece of paper, in their own words, their view of your current strategy, and then asked them to read it out loud, how would that go?"

The CEO either smiles or frowns and admits that everybody would give me a different answer. And they're right—that's exactly what happens. If there are six people on the leadership team, I get six answers. Sometimes I don't even get strategies but outcomes. Their barrier to growth, that execution problem, exists because everyone's executing on a different strategy. So we need to get everyone on the same page, beginning with the organization's strategy.

The reason no one's on the same page to begin with is usually because the CEO never communicated his strategy to any of them. Leaders may have fantastic ideas for how to run their businesses, but they need to get it out of their heads instead of assuming everyone else just knows what they're thinking. They have to get clear on the strategy, communicate it to their team in a way they understand it, and optimally, document it. Put it in writing so that if anyone ever wants to know your strategy, they can point to it and say, "This is it. This is our strategy."

THE INFLECTION POINT: UNHINGED

Reell Precision Manufacturing makes hinges, among other things. The company treats its people well and provides great employee benefits. Reell strives to put out high-quality hinges suitable for products where the hinge really matters. Years ago, the company's growth stalled, so they got into the laptop business.

Laptops were quickly becoming a commodity though, and the only way Reell could compete was to cut costs. This meant sacrificing quality. The company's revenue grew, but the people who worked there weren't happy putting out products that weren't built to the standard of their other products. Reell didn't have the cash it used to, either, and so the people weren't being taken care of, and the best people left.[24]

Reell later rebounded, but that's not how it always ends for businesses that sacrifice quality for cost. Companies go out of business all the time, and we don't always know why. So we blame it on this or that. The market. The economy. Those may have been contributing factors, but the inflection point is usually something else. If you look back far enough, you'll find a decision or a set of decisions that signaled the beginning of the end.

---

24 Bo Burlingham, *Small Giants: Companies That Choose to Be Great Instead of Big*, (New York: Portfolio, 2016).

HAVE A BHAG

People expect a lot from their leaders; they want to know where their leaders are taking them. They want to know where they're going, why they're going there, and their role in all of it. They need direction, a destination, and some context so they understand why they're showing up every day, beyond the paycheck. This is to your benefit, because if they trust you and understand where you're going, they will be thinking about how they can help you get further, faster.

Within the vivid vision, give your people a BHAG—big hairy audacious goal. The BHAG is the North Star, the Core Destination. Reaching that BHAG equals success. The goal may take decades to reach. But when you all get there, you'll be able to look at what you accomplished and say, "We did it. We set this audacious goal for ourselves and made it happen."

You don't get to that goal just any old way. You navigate with a core purpose, a reason for moving toward the goal. And you maintain core values, which are the rules that guide how you interact with one another and how you do business. Think of the BHAG as a lighthouse in the distance. You can go right for it, with no purpose or values, but you're probably going to hit some big rocks and sink, or you could plow into the beach and wreck your boat. On your voyage, you will have to make decisions and you'll look to your purpose and values to guide you. Remember Reell? They violated a core value and came to regret it years later, when it almost cost them their business.

While you're staying true to your purpose and values, you need to keep moving toward that lighthouse. That's how you grow. If you're not growing, you're shrinking—to use the boat metaphor, you're sinking. All the other businesses are out there on the water navigating toward lighthouses too, and you have to keep up with them.

This is why you need a direction, but it relies on all these other things—vivid vision, core purpose, core values—to get you further, faster and without sinking your own boat. Establish your direction. Know who you are and what's important to you, your employees, and your customers. Hold true to your values and purpose, and row toward the lighthouse.

GET UP AND STRETCH: BIG HAIRY AUDACIOUS GOAL

The BHAG comes from you, the leader. Take some time to really think about what you want your BHAG to be. It helps to make it scary—not terrifying, but scary enough that it's a stretch. That making it happen would be pretty life-shattering, but in a good way. The BHAG is impactful. It's major. Don't underestimate what you can achieve with your BHAG. If it doesn't frighten you a little, you're not going big enough.

The timeframe for achieving it could be ten years, could be thirty. It's not a goal you're going to reach this year. It's also not a goal that aligns with your current progress, so you can't just extrapolate what you're doing now into the future and call that your BHAG.

It does have to align with what your core customers want and value. It speaks to your core competencies, so it's in line with whatever you do really well. The BHAG also has to line up with your economic engine—your "profit per X." Southwest's economic engine is "Profit per Plane." Your X could be how many gadgets you sell or services you provide. It could be anything, but it has to make you money.

Write about your BHAG. Get clear on it. Set it aside and sleep on it, then look at it again. Tweak it, set it aside, look at it again, and when you're feeling like you've got it, bring it to your leadership team and see what they think.

If you're struggling with this, talk to your team about it and ask them each to come up with their own BHAG. Then get together to discuss all their ideas. You might have one real winner in the group, or you might end up combining two or more to get the best BHAG.

Compare the goal against your purpose, your passion, your core customers' wants and what they value from you, and your core competencies. Does your BHAG fit? *Does it drive your economic engine?*

Beyond revenue, will it make you cash? Will going for that BHAG make you enough profit per X, keeping in mind that you can get there with a low margin and a lot of X's or a high margin and fewer X's—to generate revenue and put cash in your reserves?

Find your BHAG. Discuss it. Tear holes in it. Make it solid and make it a goal that scares people and makes them want to rally around it. Communicate it on a regular basis so no one loses sight of it.

For a detailed description of this exercise, check out the *Further, Faster Resources* at https://catalystgrowthadvisors.com/catalyst-growth-advisors/further-faster-resources/.

THE CONTAINER STORE REVISITED

Being part of something bigger than yourself is what Kip Tindell provided for his employees at The Container Store. At any other store, customers are handed their bag and told to have a nice day. Container Store people will walk you out to the parking lot and help you load your car.

That kind of behavior isn't just good for the people who work for you, it's a marketing tool. Companies that get their people involved in a purpose spend less on marketing per dollar than most other companies. Getting people to trust you and embrace this shared purpose changes the culture, but it takes time. Once it starts, the momentum builds and the enthusiasm spreads. People talk about what they're doing to further the BHAG, and the passion is contagious. Finally, perhaps the best side effect is that people are happier and more fulfilled working like this. They enjoy coming to work knowing they can use their brains and make decisions that are good for the customer and the company. So the attrition rate is much lower. In an industry known for high turnover, The Container Store's turnover rate is in the single digits. Some employees have been there for more than thirty years.

KEY TAKEAWAY

Hire great people who believe what you believe. Tell them exactly what their success looks like and how to measure it. Support them along the way with training and an environment that welcomes ideas and invites feedback. Do this, and you will be amazed by how much they'll do for you without you ever asking them.

Your job as a leader is not to give answers, but to provide direction and allow others to find the answers. Remember when we talked about your A-team? Think about how it would be if everyone was contributing in a massive way. Instead of pulling your people along, they're pulling you forward. Create that safe place for your people. Show them your vision and invite them in. Allow them to bring value to the customer and the business. They'll be happier and stay longer, and you will have less to do.

While the high-level strategy we've established thus far gives your further, faster initiative structure, the linchpin of that strategy is your customer. Understanding your core customers and what they want and value is the subject of the next chapter.

GET UP AND STRETCH

Supporting information, exercises, worksheets, and bonus content are available at *Further, Faster Resources*, https://catalystgrowthadvisors.com/catalyst-growth-advisors/further-faster-resources/, including the following:

- **BHAG Exercise**

CHAPTER 7

//////////////////

KNOW YOUR CORE CUSTOMERS (AND WHAT THEY VALUE) BETTER THAN THEY KNOW THEMSELVES

Experience keeps a dear school, but fools will learn in no other.

—BENJAMIN FRANKLIN

You have to get so close to your customer that you know what they want before they do.

—STEVE JOBS

Google thought they were in the maps business. They were for a while, and they put MapQuest out of business because Google Maps looked better and was easier to use than MapQuest. But people don't just use maps because they look good or are easy to use—the maps have to solve a problem, and one of the reasons people were using MapQuest and Google Maps was to get from one place to another as quickly as possible. They wanted to be on time. So Google added new functionalities, like time estimates. Then there was traffic to deal with, so they took that into account and estimated your arrival time based on available traffic information. Traffic changed, though, and the estimates weren't reliable.

Then along came Waze. They didn't think of themselves as being in the maps business; they wanted to help people get from Point A to Point B and arrive on time. By now, smartphones were ubiquitous. Every person on the road had a phone, and they came with tools that might be useful to a company trying to help people navigate their way around town. An accelerometer or gyroscope, for instance. So they thought about how they use those tools to connect people looking for ways to get somewhere. Their product, the Waze app, uses a map, but no one uses it like a map. You just listen to it and it tells you where and when to turn, and how far and how long you are from your destination. The information it uses is gathered and updated in real time from all those phones.

Waze had looked at the customers' real problem and solved it. And eventually Google bought them for more than a billion dollars.

Someday I hope they add a parking function—leveraging future technology such as sensor nanotechnology in pavement that pings the app—because I can spend hours driving around Boston looking for a spot. Like other people whose problems haven't been solved, I use a workaround—driving to the perimeter, parking, and taking the subway in. But one of these days someone will invent a feature that guides you to that perfect parking spot as part of a Waze-like app. A guy can dream, right?

KNOW YOUR CUSTOMERS

The lesson for us, and for Google, is not to fall in love with your idea. Your customers will decide whether it's any good or not. Like Mike Tyson says, "A plan is great until you get punched in the face." That's what your customers will do—not literally, but you'll feel it—when they don't like your plan or your product.

You can prevent some of this pain by first taking the time to know your customers.

Knowing your customer is difficult when you don't even know who your customer is. That's a common problem with most startups. I worked at ten different startups and noticed that the original idea was not the one we ended up with for the five successful ones. The others focused too much on the original idea, and they either died eventually, or continue to struggle. Startups with this issue that survive either got very lucky, or they had enough money in the bank to get it wrong over and over again until they got it right. A few figure this out sooner because they set out to do just that.

Customers have struggles and problems, and if we don't know what those are, we can't know how to solve them. More often, we come up with a product without first considering the customer, and we expect people to like it. The product might solve some of their problem, or it may solve all of the problem for a very small constituency. In which case, you will never make a business out of that product. You have to continuously talk to your customers to understand their struggles versus creating a product and then convincing them why they should use it. Ultimately, you want them to say, "I've been trying to solve this problem for a long time—how did you get in my head and solve it for me? Thank you!"

GET UP AND STRETCH: YOUR
CUSTOMER'S VALUE PROPOSITION

The next time you meet with your team, ask them to describe, in their own words, what your customer value proposition is.

As each person gives you their answers, listen for whether they first mention themselves and their (your) company or if they focus on the *customer's* company. If the team member begins with something like, "They love us because we do (fill in the blank) well..." then they are off-base. Mark that down as a "W" for *We*. But if the team member says, "(Fill in the blank) is very important to this customer, and we were able to help them achieve this by..." then they are seeing the value proposition from the customer's point of view and you can mark that down as a "T" for *Them*.

Next, count up the Ws and Ts. Don't be surprised if the majority of your people start by talking about your business—the Ws.

When I do this exercise with my clients, that's the usual outcome. Then I have to politely tell them that their customers don't care about *what you do*; they only care about what you do *does for them*. The customer value proposition starts and ends with how you solve the customer's problems and make their lives easier and better.

People get this, but they don't *really* get it. Not right away. So ask them, "Who has a best friend? Raise your hand." Everyone raises their hand, and then I ask, "Why are they your best friend?"

They give me an assortment of answers, but the bottom line is, your best friend is your best friend because they *get* you. They know what you think about things.

That's what your customers want from you. They want you to

know what they're thinking. To know what your customers are thinking, you have to care about them. You have to show compassion. You have to be curious about their key struggles. Most importantly, you have to understand what job they are hiring your product or service to do for them.

Getting to know what your customers' problems are and what they value takes compassion. To me, compassion is empathy with action. You have to put yourself in their shoes and act upon what you discover to help them.

This doesn't mean you don't make sales or hit your numbers. That still has to happen, but it's easier if you choose to focus on your customers instead of the money. Acting in the interest of the client might take longer in the beginning, but will get you further, faster in the long run.

Knowing your customers takes conversations. People don't usually talk to their customers enough, or they only talk to them when they want to make a sale. So they ask the customer what they need, and the customer tells them. The problem is, your customer doesn't really *know* what they need. Figuring out what they need from you is not their job—it's yours. The only way to do that is to get them to tell you their problems, and like everyone else in the world, your customers will love to tell you their problems. It's what we humans enjoy more than almost anything else: complaining. And for you, that's where all the magic is. You can take all that information and come up with a solution. That's what the Waze people did. That's what The Container Store people did. They didn't look at what people were settling for, they looked at what their real problem was, and they built a solution that their customers not only wanted and needed but valued. Customers want and need many things, but they only pay for what they value.

If you ask enough customers what their problems are and what you do for them that they value, you'll begin to see a pattern. That commonality is what you need to focus on. Those are the differentiators that no one else has put together and that your customer values. It's why they buy from you and will *continue* to choose you over the competition.

GRAY MATTERS: FORCES OF PROGRESS

In his book *The Forces of Progress*, author Kobus van der Zel explains the emotional forces that generate and shape customers' demand for a product.

The first group contains Push (e.g., circumstances surrounding the current situation such as an old lawnmower that is difficult to push around the lawn) and Pull (e.g., seeing your neighbor with a new lawnmower that pulls the operator forward automatically), or the forces that work together to *generate* demand. The other group is Habit (e.g., "My existing lawnmower is fine; I can go another year with it") and Anxiety (e.g., "What if I can't figure out how to control it? I might look silly as my neighbor looks on"), or the forces that work together to *reduce* demand. Customers experience some combination of these forces—often all at once—as they search for, choose, purchase, and use a product to make their lives better.

It is important for leaders to understand what is driving their customers to move toward a decision to purchase and what forces may be stopping them. There may be market demand that is yet unaccounted for or hidden objections your salespeople don't even know to address. These hidden objections are often masked by the ever-popular, "The price is too high" or "We are just not ready to move ahead yet."

For instance, Bob was in the business of selling condos. His Core Customers were empty nesters. Before building the condo complex, he asked some folks who wanted to move to a smaller footprint home (Push) what was important to them in a condo so he could design something that they would be happy with (Pull). He was told that one-floor living, a second bedroom for guests and grandchildren, and a few other items were important. Bob built the units to these specifications and early on, many sold. However, soon his sales stalled. There were many interested parties but they were not moving forward. After many discovery interviews, he kept hearing something about the dining room table. He found that many people and couples were ready to move but would not do so until they figured out what to do with the dining room table—and these newly designed units didn't have room for the table. For these people, the table held a certain reverence since there were so many memories associated with it. They could not just throw it out. With this information, Bob redesigned future units by shrinking the second bedroom to create more space for the dining room table. Sales shot up and stayed there.

Bob was unaware of the unspoken anxiety a large number of potential buyers had before they would move ahead. He had done a great job of the push and pull pieces but had not looked for reasons some folks had for not moving such as the dining room table or, as he also discovered, what they would do with all of the stuff they had in the attic and basement. When he solved for the latter by adding a "sorting room," he got another permanent jump in sales.[25]

This is what I mean when I say Know Your Customers. Since we are primarily emotional creatures, we have to apply logical and emotional constructs to the marketing process.

YOUR CORE CUSTOMERS

Core customers are profitable because they value what

---

25   Kobus van der Zel, *The Forces of Progress: A Journey in Search of the Primary Forces that Either Fuel or Destroy Progress in Companies Today* (Morrisville: Lulu, 2011).

you offer and will pay more for it. They are happy to buy from you, and they generally make great references. Plenty of other customers will buy from you but require so much attention that the profit is marginal, or they irritate your people so much, they affect morale and productivity.

Your core customers love doing business with you and you with them. They require fewer resources and are high-margin customers, leaving you with more resources and more money to improve your company. These customers value something specific—*your core competencies that you do better than anyone else and set you apart from competitors and that you apply to a solution that meets or exceeds your customers' expectations.*

Some customers will value other things you do, but these are not your core customers. Trying to serve them will take away from what you're doing for your core, drain your resources, and inevitably pull you apart into two or more different companies. You can spin off a new business, but that's not how you move your current company further, faster. You need to focus on what you do best that your best customers value and will pay for to get there. Grow that market and you'll grow your business. You don't need all the market, either: Apple, at one time, with just 7 percent of their market share, had 70 percent of the profit share.

There's also value in referrals, and there's value in customer loyalty because you're not having to shell out a lot of money for customer acquisition. So your marketing budget for cost per unit is going to be less. Core customers are loyal and they prefer to upgrade rather than switching to something totally new, so you have repeat business locked in.

Companies who forget the value of their core customers like to create shiny new things to attract new business, sacrificing their core customers in the process. It behooves us to focus more deeply on our best customers and understand why they buy from us.

You will have many conversations with customers, and most of them won't tell you what you need to know. Listen closely, because once in a while they will tell you why they buy from you. They may not even be aware of the reason themselves, but it will come out. This is what you focus on—not personas, or demographics, or anything else in your marketing database. That's great for building lists and marketing campaigns, but it should not drive your product development. It's not why people buy from you.

GET UP AND STRETCH: HOW TO DESIGN A SOLUTION THAT YOUR BEST CUSTOMERS WANT AND VALUE

I believe that knowing your customer is *the* single most important external element that drives your strategy. Strategy is about choice—what you choose to do and more importantly, what you choose not to do in order to succeed* in the marketplace. To figure out these choices, you must understand what your core customer truly wants and values. Another way to say it is, you must understand the Job to be Done.

When I first started as VP of Sales at a data backup company called LiveVault, I asked the existing team why our customers buy from us. I was told that we are in the business of selling "insurance." That is, our customers wanted an insurance policy in case they lost their data for some reason. This sounded like a pretty good answer as it was not about what we did, but what the customer valued. They were willing to pay us a monthly fee to automatically backup their data every few minutes and store it on our servers so it could be easily and quickly retrieved should disaster strike.

However, I didn't stop there. I wanted to hear directly from our customers. During my first few weeks, I interviewed about twenty existing customers to ask them why they bought from us. What I heard was a completely different story than I heard from the LiveVault team.

I spoke primarily to owners of SMBs, our main customer segment, and most of them told me the same thing in almost exactly the same words when I asked this question. "What is the most valuable thing you derived from using our service?" The answer: "Set it and forget it."

Wow! We were selling insurance but they were buying time. They were super busy and this was one less thing to worry about. They valued eliminating a boring and tedious task from their day more than whether or not they might lose data. They wanted to focus on their business. They valued the data and did not want to lose it, but this was not the primary reason for the purchase.

When the sales team began to say these five words to prospects combined with another key initiative, our business began to accelerate, rapidly culminating in an extremely high percentage of EBITDA acquisition eighteen months later.

The following exercise is a simple and easy way to check back in with your customers. This is a step you can do to more quickly get valuable data. However, it does not replace the need to continue to learn from customers directly in face-to-face interactions preferably.

The steps follow:

1. Create a list of your current customers and order them by profit (percent and/or total profit dollars). *(IMPORTANT: Your*

list should contain the name of the key decision-maker if they are still at the company, and the name of the key person who uses your product/service most often today, if they are someone other than the key decision-maker.) There are variations of this based on the complexity of the buying process so use your best judgment, remembering that the fewer people the better and one name is best.

2. Create two additional columns with the following headings:

   a. You REALLY love working with them (i.e., they are easy to work with, do not haggle on price, provide proactive referrals and are happy to provide references when asked).

   b. They REALLY love working with you (i.e., they tell you how much you have helped them in their jobs, lives, businesses, and talk about you often with others. You can hear their smile on the phone.)

3. Put an X in the column where appropriate for at least the first twenty customers.

4. Re-order the list by pushing all the customers that meet both criteria above to the top. Maintain the profit order.

5. Move to the one-question process below.

Ask One Question

Creating this list of your best customers, in and of itself, may be illuminating. However, it also is the list of people to whom you will ask one critical question. Here is what you do next:

Craft an email to the people you listed for each company for at least the top twenty customers on the list and ask the following:

Dear XXXXXX,

Thank you for being a great customer. We value your business and your input to help us continually improve. To that end, we would be grateful for your reply to this email guided by the following request.

If you were to send a short note to a trusted colleague who would receive a similar positive outcome(s) by working with our products/services, what would you say to them? Please be sure to include the following information:

1. *The most valuable thing that you (and your team) get from doing business with us, (i.e., how we helped you with a current struggle and how they might feel once we helped to make things easier or better for them as well) and,*

2. ***(Bonus future-proofing question)*** *If you had a magic wand where anything was possible, what else would you want us to provide to you and how that would make things easier or better for you (and your team)? Please be as specific as you can.*

When the answers start to come back, it is highly likely that you will start to see a pattern and get some new ideas on how you can add even more value to your best customers.

From this information, you can do a number of things. Here are some suggestions:

1. Modify your offering to get much better at what your best customers value.

2. Eliminate or minimize some of the things that they do not value and are costly for you to provide.

3. With permission, use their replies as testimonials in your marketing and sales efforts.

4. Create a target list of future customers that you think are much like the top names on this list, including those already with competitors.

5. Train your salespeople to start saying the words that you read in these notes when talking to future prospects.

6. Consider firing the customers at the very bottom of the list as you may be losing money or making little to no profit from them. They are very likely taking valuable time and resources away from your most profitable customers and affecting employee engagement. (*IMPORTANT: You must create this*

list for ALL current customers for this part).

7. If not established already, have the leadership team cultivate a relationship with the key decision-makers at your top customers that drive 80 percent or more of your profit. They are the lifeblood of your business!

8. Have your product people talk to/observe these users to get ideas on how you can improve the experience.

9. Contact the names on the list to get further clarification, when necessary, as to what they want and value the most.

10. Ask for the names and permission to contact the trusted colleagues they were thinking of.

11. Create your Core Customer sentence that describes the common three to five key attributes and what they want and value the most from working with you. For instance, "Our core customer is an extremely busy, small or medium business owner between the ages of thirty-five to fifty that greatly values their data and are looking for data-backup solutions where they can "Set it and forget it." Communicate this sentence in such a way that if I walked up to any team member at random, they could recite it off the top of their head.

If you come up with more ways that this information could be helpful, please share them with me at bill@catalystgrowthadvisors.com.

You can find a template for this exercise at: https://cat-alystgrowthadvisors.com/catalyst-growth-advisors/further-faster-resources/.

*Adapted from John Wooden's definition of success: *Peace of mind attained only through self-satisfaction in knowing you made the effort to do the best of which you're capable to grow your business, yourself and your team.*[26]

KEY TAKEAWAY

Figure out the job your customer hires your products and services to do for them. Talk to your most profitable customers often. Ask them to share their struggles. Encourage them to complain. Interview your customers like you are a journalist with no stake in the outcome. The magic is in the emotional words you hear. Explore those deeply. You will be surprised by what you learn. They will think you can read their minds and will reward you handsomely for it.

Don't solve for the immediate—the quick, one-time sale. Solve for the long-term. Solve for the people for whom you've created the best answer to their problem. Solve for the many who value you enough to pay more, without expecting the moon. Solve for those customers who will

---

26 John Wooden, with Steve Jamison, *Wooden: A Lifetime of Observations and Reflections On and Off the Court* (New York: McGraw-Hill, 1997).

buy from you over and over again because you've cared enough to learn who they are and what they really need.

Adopt a compassionate mindset. This isn't about manipulation. It's about empathy and action. You have a vivid vision, a core purpose, and core values. This is how you live all of that and how your business fulfills its destiny.

Shifting to this mindset isn't an easy thing, especially if you're used to being the smartest person in the room. You're used to knowing more than everyone else, but when it comes to what your customers truly value, you very likely don't know. Humble yourself and listen— really *listen*.

The customer is the center of your everything, including your strategy. Get the core customer right, and your strategy and everything that follows will be built on that strong core. Without this, you can build a successful small business. But if you want to get further, faster, start with the customer. Always. They are the linchpin that will launch you to a winning strategy, the topic of the next chapter.

GET UP AND STRETCH

Supporting information, exercises, worksheets, and bonus content are available at *Further, Faster Resources*, https://catalystgrowthadvisors.com/catalyst-growth-advisors/further-faster-resources/, including the following:

- **Core Customer Blog Post Link**

CHAPTER 8

KEY STRATEGIES

You have to choose what you suck at.

—FRANCES FREI (PARAPHRASED)

Southwest Airlines decided they were going to suck at a number of things. They weren't going to be good at frequent flyer benefits or membership rewards. They weren't going to be good at seat selection, first class, or inflight meals. They weren't even going to be good at airports, because some were more expensive than others. All of those choices about what Southwest was not going to be good at made it inconvenient for customers, but they were conscious choices the airline made so they could focus on being really good at other things. They decided to excel at low fares, lots of flight choices, and lots of fun. To do that, they had to forego the amenities offered by airlines that cost more, had fewer choices, and probably weren't as much fun for passengers.

Southwest keeps its costs down in ways that are inconvenient to employees too. When you're getting off one of their planes, the flight attendants are already cleaning up behind you instead of waiting for everyone to depart. That saves time, so when the last person leaves the plane, the next round of passengers can start filing in.

Other airlines have tried to copy Southwest, but none have been able to repeat what they do or their success. Southwest created a set of interdependent activities that protects them from competitors, and they didn't do it by going head-to-head with airlines who could do food, seating, or airports better than they could.

STRATEGY

When I talk to people about strategy, they typically respond with, "So, it's like a plan, right?" Not exactly.

A *plan* is about *doing*. *Strategy* is about *thinking*.

Strategy can seem like an abstract concept, but it doesn't have to be. Basically, it's about understanding your customer really well: knowing what they value and don't value so you can decide what *not* to do. Strategy is thinking about what makes you unique too.

My definition of strategy starts with Harvard Business

School professor Michael Porter's definition of competitive strategy, in short, "About being different...It means deliberately choosing a different set of activities to deliver a unique mix of value"[27] but I expanded on it based on Ford and Boeing exec Alan Mulally's take on what customers value. I define strategy as "a unique position incorporating a differentiating set of interdependent activities producing solutions our core customers want and value."

Three words in that rather long definition are critical: unique, interdependent, and value.

Unique, because when it comes to strategy, different *and* better is best, but different is *always* better than better.

When you're better, everyone will figure out what you do and copy it. You're running this high-speed marathon that never ends. It's working super hard just to stay ahead of your competition, sometimes throwing more bodies at whatever needs to be done as opposed to doing fewer things more effectively and efficiently, which is only possible when you focus on *different*. But that uniqueness isn't just one thing; it's a set of interdependent activities that you do well enough to give you an impenetrable strategy.

---

27   Michael E. Porter, "What Is Strategy?" *Harvard Business Review*, November–December 1996, https://hbr.org/1996/11/what-is-strategy.

Interdependent, because doing that different thing really well through a combination of key actions and activities creates a moat around your business that is very difficult if not impossible to cross. That combination adds up to something unique that your core customers truly value. Southwest made decisions about where they flew from, how they loaded planes, and the culture they wanted to create. They hired people for their personalities and offered low fares. That interdependence among features added up to success.

You have to choose what not to do as well as what to do because strategy is primarily about choice—choosing what you excel at versus what you suck at.

Value, because your core customers care a lot about a small percentage of what your product or service does for them, and care very little about the rest of it. So instead of adding more bells and whistles, think about how you can strip down the design to the few things your core customers value most and do *those* really well.

What your customers value isn't always obvious. They will tell you what they want, but they won't always be willing to pay for what they want. They will pay for what they value.

> **Strategy**: A **unique** market position incorporating a differenti-
> ating set of **interdependent** activities producing solutions our
> core customers want and **value**.

Unique. Interdependent. Value. Use them to set you apart.
People will naturally compare you with all other companies that do what you do—give them a reason to look
beyond prices to what you do really well that they value.

The essence of strategy is getting into your customer's
head and understanding their struggles and what they're
doing today to try to solve them. Are you asking your
customers what they want? Well, you'll never get the
right answer doing that. Because you and I both know
that your customer may *want* something but wanting it
doesn't guarantee they're going to be willing to *pay* for
it. Unless they truly value it, you'll end up spending a lot
of money building a product that no one wants to pay
for—or pay *more* for.

Whether you compete with a "low-price" strategy like
Southwest, Walmart, and McDonald's, or with a "joy to
use" strategy like Apple, Dyson, or Nest, have a strategy.
And don't settle for being in the middle. Companies that
do that get squeezed in one direction or the other, and
they don't always survive. Blockbuster, Nokia, BlackBerry,
and Kodak all thought the customer wanted what they

made, when they should have been asking their customers what they valued.

INTERNAL/EXTERNAL ANALYSIS

In chapter 6 we talked about your BHAG (Big Hairy Audacious Goal), which is that big goal you want to accomplish ten years out—maybe longer. Now let's think about other goals, ones that people can get their heads around more easily. What *you* can accomplish in three years. Shannon Susko refers to this as your 3HAG™, the Three-Year Highly Achievable Goal.[28]

Work with your team to identify your 3HAG. Start with a date three years in the future, we'll say December 31, 202X. Then imagine what that day will look like for your company. Paint a picture of what you *want* that day to look like. Write down your financial metrics on that date. Where are you on revenue, profits, cash, and maybe gross margin?

Compare that picture with where you are now. Then figure out how you're going to get where you want to be on December 31, 202X.

The picture doesn't have to be about just money. Your goal

---

28 Shannon Byrne Susko, *3HAG Way: The Strategic Execution System that ensures your strategy is not a Wild-Ass-Guess!* (Vancouver: Ceozen Consulting Inc., 2018).

might be to have stronger teams. So within three years, you need to invest in building better teams by improving your hiring, training, and ongoing team support. Creating strong teams won't happen overnight, but you can do this in three years. You will have to learn how to attract the best people for your teams, how to interview them, and how to onboard them. You'll have to improve your skills training. You might have to put some real effort into helping people lay out a career path. You'll also have to learn how to better exit employees too. The company will outgrow people, and other people will outgrow the company.

Talk with your team about their ideas for potential 3HAGs. Have everyone weigh in and see what makes the most sense. When I do this with businesses, there is often a huge gap in ambition. The CEO usually sets his sights highest with lofty goals that might seem too difficult to everyone else, while others want to set goals that you may find too easy to achieve. If you're at $10 million in revenue now, you might want to be at $30 million in three years, while your VP of Sales wants to hit just $12 million. Consider what's achievable, not what's easy. You may have to adjust your expectations. If most of your people agree that the goal is achievable, then set it. If you truly believe it's achievable and no one else does, you might have a problem with your team.

GET UP AND STRETCH: SET YOUR 3HAG

Asking your team these questions will help you figure out the best Three-Year Highly Achievable Goal for your business.

1. What future date will we choose for our 3HAG?

2. What are our fiscal measurements?

3. How many widgets do we have to make to hit those numbers?

Say you're at $5 million in revenue right now. You set your 3HAG to $20 million, which means you have to increase revenue by $5 million a year in three years. If the average widget price is $500, then you will need to make 40,000 widgets in year three to generate that kind of revenue.

The widget is basically the output from sales to operations. This could be orders, projects, or something else—whatever generates a sale and brings in money. It could be a single product.

1. How can we describe our 3HAG statement of where our company will be in three years *without using numbers*? This is hard to do because in business we tend to think in numbers. What will the company look like if you're making $10 million three years from now? What will it be like for your people and for your employees? Paint that picture. This is what you will be striving for internally and is often a short-term step to your

BHAG. If you have a BHAG of "being the biggest and best in the industry," your 3HAG external view might be "being the biggest and the best in the country," for example.

2. Now that we've figured out when and what the measurements are and how many widgets we need to sell, what three to five key capabilities will we need to master in order to get there? This might be improving human resource systems, adopting new technologies, building a factory, or inventing a new product. It could be anything that gets you to that goal. What do we want to be known for? What do we want our customers, our competitors, and the media to say about us in three years? This is the external view of the business.

3. Use this 3HAG to focus on the key objectives you need to meet to build a moat around your business that no one can cross and that will deliver your goal in your timeframe. At one of Susko's companies, Paradata, her "known for" was the following: *Make PAYMENTS easy.*

For more on the 3HAG exercise, including a graphic depiction of creating a strategy execution system, visit https://catalystgrowthadvisors.com/catalyst-growth-advisors/further-faster-resources/.

Susko's books *The Metronome Effect* and *3HAG Way* include a number of supporting exercises that enhance the 3HAG questions. These include the following:

- The "Stakeholder" MAP: What is the arena you are playing in?
- Attribution Framework: Where is the white space in your industry?
- Activity Fit Map I and II: What are the key differentiators you need to win?
- Swimlanes: What is the three-year plan to implement your 3HAG strategy?
- Thirty-six-month Key Business Metrics Rolling Forecast: Detailed forecast for Revenue, Profit, Cash, Widgets and People
- Brand Promise and Guarantee: What promise will you make to make it easier for your core customers to choose you?
- Secret Sauce: What difficult industry problem can you solve that will accelerate your growth with high velocity?

Susko's website, https://metronomeunited.com, also covers the topics, and I am one of many coaches around the globe who can help you take these more advanced steps to go even further, and faster.

KEY TAKEAWAY

It is your job as Head of Company to get the leadership team on the same page when it comes to strategy. If they cannot simply and clearly articulate your strategy with one voice, the rest of the organization will be stumbling around in the darkness with a candle. This simple act will increase cohesiveness and productivity everywhere with everyone.

Figure out your core customer, create a strategy, and set your 3HAG. Give your people some real, tangible goals to sink their teeth into that they can reach within three years. When you identify what your customer truly wants and values, and you do what you love and are great at that drives your economic engine for a large enough part of the market, there's almost no size you can't become. Your only choice then is, how big you want to be and how fast you want to get there. You've taken the guesswork out of growth, not because you're a genius predictor— but because you are now *controlling* your growth. You know what it takes to grow: how many people you need, how many products you need to make, and the activities and costs required for that growth. You can make informed decisions about how far and how fast you can go—and grow.

Strategy is about thinking. Now it's time to act.

GET UP AND STRETCH

Supporting information, exercises, worksheets, and bonus content are available at *Further, Faster Resources*, https://catalystgrowthadvisors.com/catalyst-growth-advisors/further-faster-resources/, including the following:

- **3HAG Questions**
- **3HAG Priorities**

CHAPTER 9

EXECUTE YOUR STRATEGIES

Resolve to perform what you ought; perform without fail what you resolve.

—BENJAMIN FRANKLIN

When you first learned to drive a car, you had to think about every action because they weren't habits yet. You thought about where you put the key, where the pedals were, and how much to turn the wheel. You trained yourself to look for traffic lights, signs, cars, and people on the road. Eventually, driving a car became habitual and you didn't have to think about it anymore. Then you thought about other things, like listening to the radio or talking to passengers—activities that required conscious thought to execute safely while you drove.

Execution of any kind requires habits. To scale your business, you have to develop habits that get you further. When you practice habits in your business, you're letting people know, "This is how we do these things—what we do, how we do it, and when we do it." The repetition creates discipline for your people and your business. Habits create discipline, and discipline drives performance. Again, you have to fire yourself from the day-to-day, and to do that, you have to get everyone on the right track, doing what needs to be done to grow the business so you're not doing all of it yourself.

What habits will you practice and instill in your people? First and foremost, those habits that get you further, faster. The ones that make your people, your teams, and your business stronger and more sustainable and allow you to achieve your 3HAG and eventually, your BHAG.

Make them first and foremost—prioritize them. Priorities, metrics, and meetings drive execution and make your plan for growth actually happen. Set the priorities, measure your progress, and talk about them in meetings to keep them top of mind for your leadership team and their teams.

You can have the best strategy in the world but if you don't execute on it, it won't work. On the other hand, you can execute on a half-decent strategy and still beat everyone else. Executed well, your strategy's flaws will be apparent and you can make adjustments. Executing on this idea is a process of continuous improvement, where you're executing, experiencing varying degrees of success, and tweaking the strategy based on what you learn.

Like a flywheel, as your strategy is executed and refined, it gains momentum and becomes easier to maintain. As people develop the habits to keep the flywheel spinning, you can begin to separate yourself from the day-to-day running of the operation to spend more time figuring out what the future will look like for the business.

1HAG, KEY METRICS, AND SMAART GOALS

After you prioritize your activities within the 3HAG (Three-Year Highly Achievable Goal), create a *One*-Year Highly Achievable Goal, or 1HAG plan that defines what you can accomplish in the next year. Just like with the BHAG (Big Hairy Audacious Goal), set a date, fiscal measures, and any other outcomes or markers of success in achieving that goal.

Then establish key metrics that show your current status and future progress moving toward that One-Year Highly Achievable Goal. Determine what you need to do to reach those metrics, prioritize them, and assign owners to them. Don't get too complicated with this—one to five key metrics is plenty. Often, fewer is better.

This is a simple but important exercise because it's basically a subset of your 3HAG, so you've already done the heavy lifting. You'll be tempted to want to look at too many key indicators and measure too many metrics but try to focus on as few as possible. If you have five metrics, is there one metric that encompasses all of them?

You've no doubt heard of SMART goals. Your priorities and metrics should be SMART, too, except I call mine SMAART, with two As: Specific, Measurable, Achievable, *Authority*, Relevant, and Time-Based. The second A is for Authority because the person responsible has to have the authority to get it done. If you assign someone a priority, they need to have the right to do it without having to ask permission from someone else. If another person typically has the authority, they need to temporarily relinquish authority to the owner of the priority.

GET UP AND STRETCH: PRIORITIES AND OWNERSHIP

Everyone on the leadership team has to commit to the company's #1 1HAG priority. Have each person write this down independently and bring it to a meeting where you discuss and agree on one single top priority from the choices, or from a combination of the choices.

Once you've all agreed, remind everyone that if they have any misgivings, this is their chance to speak up because it's going to be the company's main focus for the next year. Everyone has to actually say, "Yes, I believe this should be our #1 priority" or "No, I do not, and here's why." Have that conversation now and get everyone's opinions on the table. Even if you have people who do not agree, they need to be heard and they also need to ultimately commit to the common goal, which may turn out to be different than the original one. It is important that everyone understand what being the #1 priority means. That is, the team will sacrifice individual activities if the #1 priority is at risk and all other priorities are subservient to the #1 priority if necessary.

If you have your meetings in the same room every week, have your function-organizational chart, key process flow map, and 3HAG visible to remind people what you are all working toward and who's responsible for every part of making it happen. You might have all this in digital format, but you don't want people staring at their laptops during this discussion, so it's better to have these items on the wall. They don't have to be fancy—they just have to be legible. Having all of this in view can spark a new thought, a priority that no one brought to the table. This is everyone's chance to explore those ideas.

After you decide on the first priority, discuss your options for the second, and if you have them, the third, fourth, and fifth priorities.

After you've identified the priorities, ask your team who owns each one. Write their name on it. To make this easy, I use an easel and a big pad of easel sheets that you can stick on the wall. Your team needs to take this ownership seriously and be willing to say out loud, "I own that. It's mine!" They can't volunteer other people or begrudgingly accept nomination for it either. They have to want to do it. If more than one person wants to own a priority, then ask each person to defend why it should be theirs.

Do this with your 1HAG and with quarterly goals within the plan. Then discuss the more granular, individual priorities that each person owns. This might be a goal or an initiative within their own teams. At the end of the meeting, each person should have three to five priorities comprising 1HAG goals, quarterly goals, and individual team initiatives—all with completion dates and metrics to measure progress and completion.

Determining priorities and ownership this way gets everyone involved. Your people choose the company's priorities, decide which ones they'll own, and figure out how to accomplish them.

ACCOUNTABILITY: RED, YELLOW, OR GREEN

Simplifying the 1HAG makes the process easier and more effective, but there is no silver bullet. Once you set a BHAG, a 3HAG, and a 1HAG, you can break that one-year goal into quarters (QHAG) and monitor progress closely while you and your team create and practice habits that move you toward the goal. You can also break it down by week, if your team consistently misses these priorities. Meet regularly to check in on everyone's progress.

When I talk with people about progress, I don't want to get into a lot of the details because frankly, they don't concern me and spending time in the weeds isn't a good use of our time. I just want to check in with them: Here's what we decided needed to be done and here's our timeline for doing it. Where are we with it? We all know the priorities and who owns them. So I call on each owner and ask them the question, "Red, yellow, or green?" Green means that they're on track or ahead of schedule. Red means the metric will not be met or will not be met within the time we set. Yellow means that the owner is concerned—the metric may or may not be met, but it's too early to tell.

Then I ask them which priority we need to talk about that day and which priorities need to be discussed among themselves at their next meeting. The owner should decide whether or not an item requires further discussion. This discussion comes after—and never before—the Good News and Weekend Reports that we talked about in chapter 1. That's everyone's opportunity to toot their own horns a little, instead of in the middle of your more serious discussions.

Once you've completed the priorities and ownership

exercise, encourage your leadership team to do the same with their individual teams. They can grab an easel and a big pad and do exactly what you did, or they can use a white board, or they can do it any way they want. But they have to get their teams involved and not just hand down orders.

GRAY MATTERS: DON'T EVERYONE TALK AT ONCE

When you work through the priorities and ownerships, have each person write their answers on sticky notes and turn them in for discussion. If you just allow a free-for-all, you'll hear from the same people you always hear from. Hearing from everyone, you'll get more ideas and, usually, better ideas.

Some people take a little longer to think, but they don't get the chance. The quick thinkers and fast talkers get their opinions out there, setting the stage for the discussion. Other ideas are left unspoken. When you want to make the most of the collective intelligence of the room, don't do it verbally—have people write down their thoughts. This also avoids anchoring. Anchoring happens when one person says something out loud and others find it difficult to think of anything else, which limits diverse input and narrows the focus too early in the discussion and decision process.

Before you send your leadership team back out to meet with

their own teams, tell them about this practice, especially those people with large teams and unofficial "leaders" who always seem to make themselves heard.

GET UP AND STRETCH: BE THE CHIEF EXPLANATION OFFICER

As you establish and document the core purpose, core values, core competencies, and BHAG of your business, document and communicate them. Make it part of your job to know and repeat these things. Write your story and your company's story and repeat it often. Your people should know why you started this business and why what you are all doing together matters.

You may have started your business as the chief executive officer, but that "e" might as well stand for "explanation." You're the chief explanation officer. Practice your story and say it enough times that people finish your sentences. That's when you know they're finally hearing you.

Money motivates people for a short time but being part of something bigger they believe in will keep them engaged for the long haul. Repeat these things in meetings and call attention to people who support them. Reward employees who reflect the core values and purpose. Thank them for moving the business closer to that big hairy audacious goal.

KEY TAKEAWAY

Execution is about habits and discipline. Flawless execution is reached by setting and accomplishing three things:

1. **Priorities**: What key activities and outcomes must we perform and achieve to bring us closer to our longer-term goals? Are they SMAART?
2. **Metrics**: How do we know when we achieved our priorities? What are the right measurements?
3. **Meetings**: Are we meeting productively to ensure we are achieving our priorities as written and on time while also running the day-to-day effectively?

In Part I, we talked about performance being a team sport. Execution is accomplished by teams, so your teams must be aligned around these goals. Communicating the goals to your teams typically happens in regular meetings, the subject of our next chapter.

GET UP AND STRETCH

Supporting information, exercises, worksheets, and bonus content are available at *Further, Faster Resources*, https://catalystgrowthadvisors.com/catalyst-growth-advisors/further-faster-resources/, including the following:

- **1HAG Priorities**
- **QHAG/90-Day Priorities**

CHAPTER 10

//////////////////////

ESTABLISH MEETING RHYTHMS AND AGENDAS

I'm sorry to imprison you in this long meeting, as I did not have time to prepare a short one.

—JIM COLLINS, "TEN LESSONS I LEARNED FROM PETER DRUCKER"[29]

According to recent studies, 50 percent of a company's time is dedicated to meetings. In fact, senior executives spend two days or more a week in a meeting, and 67 percent of them consider the meetings failures. So

---

29   Jim Collins, "Ten Lessons I Learned from Peter Drucker," *JimCollins.com*, May 17, 2016, https://www.jimcollins.com/article_topics/articles/Ten-Lessons-I-Learned-from-Peter-Drucker.html.

potentially, US businesses are wasting $37 billion a year on unproductive meetings.[30]

We've got to get better at meetings.

If you ask people if they hate meetings, they will tell you they hate meetings. I argue that people don't hate meetings, they hate boring meetings. And most meetings *are* boring because most of us aren't very good at them.

Meetings don't have to be boring and they shouldn't be.

They should never be a waste of time either, because they're expensive. Don't believe me? Calculate the average pay someone on your leadership team gets for an hour of work and multiply that times how many people you have in the room for your meeting. And that's just one hour—meetings can go on for much longer.

There are many ways to run good meetings that people won't hate but actually look forward to. Effective, productive meetings that aren't a waste of time and money. I'm going to tell you about my way, which I believe is the best way—not that I'm partial, but I've tried it this way and it works.

---

30 Dana Larsen, "Are meetings costing your business too much money?" *SAP Concur*, January 17, 2017, https://www.concur.com/newsroom/article/are-meetings-costing-your-business-too-much-money.

GRAY MATTERS: DO MORE WITH YOUR BRAIN

Our brains are wonderful: they work while we're asleep and awake, processing endless transactions per second, coming up with myriad ways to do things. They do all of this and do not stop until we arrive at work. Then, our brains' activity turns to meetings and emails, meetings and emails, meetings and emails.

Imagine what might happen if we showed up at the office free to unleash our brains' innate power. What would that feel like? What might we accomplish?

PROGRESS, NOT STATUS

The biggest, most boring use of time in a company is the Status Meeting. You've been in this meeting, or this first hour of a meeting, where everyone provides a status update. The focus is on the past—what's been accomplished. People spend time justifying their existence and value by sharing almost everything they did that week. That's what reports are for. You don't need to tell everyone what's in a report. You should have sent out the report already, and people should have read it, and if they have questions about it, well, they can ask them at the meeting.

Progress meetings are about moving forward and making adjustments. You can bring your report but you can't read it and go through it blow-by-blow. If anyone didn't read it, shame on them. It's not your job to do their homework for them. Your job is to share any piece of the report that you think is important enough for everyone or most people in the room to know about, or that you need help with from them, and should discuss in this meeting.

Changing the focus of a meeting from status to progress brings vitality to a meeting. It infuses life and gets people excited. It also forces them to prepare, because they're not going to point at a screen, regurgitating facts and figures. They have to think about the meeting.

The weekly senior leadership meeting—your million-dollar meeting—is priority #1 when it comes to fixing the meeting problem. It's costing you a lot not only in dollars, but in lost opportunities for your business.

Every company has a weekly leadership meeting, but few have a daily huddle. You need both, and you need to do them both well to take your business further, faster.

THE FURTHER, FASTER "MEETING WITH PURPOSE"

Over the years, I've developed a method for getting further, faster in meetings. This is a combination of learnings from Dave Baney, Verne Harnish, Gino Wickham, Ron Huntington, and my own experience.

Before you call a meeting, take these five steps:

1. Determine the ideal outcome of that meeting.
2. Figure out who needs to be there to make that happen.
3. Establish meeting rhythms and ground rules.
4. Have an agenda.
5. Run the meeting with purpose.

Let's talk about how you do this.

THE IDEAL MEETING OUTCOME

Ideally, a meeting's outcome achieves a result that's tied to a specific purpose aside from the smaller objectives. When each attendee understands how the meeting is connected to a larger "why," they have a greater appreciation for its necessity and are motivated to participate in achieving a favorable outcome. For instance, the daily huddle, fashioned after John D. Rockefeller's "daily practice"[31] is a way to understand what everyone's priority is that day, how they did yesterday, and where they might be stuck, along with some good news to help increase team cohesion.

The team also knows the "higher purpose" of a daily huddle:

---

31 Ron Chernow, *Titan: The Life of John D. Rockefeller, Sr.* (New York: Vintage, 2004).

1. It increases velocity.
2. It heals relationships.
3. It gets everyone on the same page.
4. It highlights problems before they become crises.

An ideal meeting outcome is accomplished by crafting the agenda in advance and sharing it with the attendees who have been carefully selected to join based on their expected contribution. Each person is expected to add value to the meeting and contribute to the best possible decision. In an ideal meeting, as we learned in chapter 2 regarding Google's Aristotle Project, everyone is heard about the same amount of time, and the team comes to a decision that can be supported *at least* 80 percent by everyone, so they all leave fully supporting the decisions made in the meeting.

The meeting's desired outcome determines who you invite and what you talk about.

INVITE THE RIGHT PEOPLE, CREATE THE RIGHT TEAM

When you schedule a meeting, only invite the people who need to be there for you to achieve your outcomes. People who are invited should be told *why* they're invited and what's expected of them so they can prepare.

Before you send out a meeting invitation, think about the

purpose of the meeting and the desired outcome. Then decide who needs to be there. Don't resort to the usual lineup: people who usually attend but don't need to be in this particular meeting surely have other work they could be doing. People who typically aren't invited maybe need to be in this one.

If you're changing up the invitee list, let people know why. Don't leave them hanging, wondering if you're talking about some secret agenda—or about them. And don't give the unintended impression that a new attendee's position has been elevated because suddenly they're in a meeting they don't usually attend. Let people know that you're adjusting the attendee lists for everyone's benefit, and for the benefit of the company. That the people who attend meetings are invited because they have to be there for you to achieve an outcome.

When you have an outcome in mind that's going to require decision-making, figure out who the stakeholders are and have them in the meeting. If they can't make the meeting then don't have the meeting or understand that you can't fully engage with the decision until the stakeholders are present. I'm a big fan of waiting and having a meeting when everyone's there who needs to be there. Otherwise, you're going to have two meetings when you could have had just one. And by the way, if you're not going to make any decisions that lead to an outcome in a meeting, you probably shouldn't be having a meeting at all. Getting a bunch of people in a room out of habit is a waste of everyone's time.

Another bad habit worth breaking is inviting entire teams to meetings when everyone on the team doesn't need to attend. Sometimes it makes more sense to have just one member in attendance to represent the team, and you can even rotate through team members so they all have an opportunity to participate—just not all at the same time. That person can then report back to their team with written notes or a verbal update at their own meeting.

Take some time to review your usual meeting rosters. Are there people who attend that don't need to be there? People who should be included but are not? How would changing those rosters alter the dynamics of the meeting, and what might be accomplished?

THE AGENDA

The agenda is the responsibility of the person who's running the meeting. This may be the same person every time, or people may take turns. That person gets the agenda out along with a message, "What did I miss?" If there's any feedback, the agenda is modified and re-sent.

If there's something on the agenda that people need to have read ahead of time, call that out so they're not caught off-guard and have time to prepare. Be fair about how much time you give them too—if they need to read an entire article or the results of a survey, don't expect them to do that the morning of the meeting, when their time is most likely already booked.

How much time you give them is really dependent on what you're doing. The daily huddle has a standard agenda and you shouldn't expect people to prepare at length for it. For the weekly meeting, people will probably need at least a day or two. For my leadership weekly meetings, I asked each department head to provide their weekly reports by five o'clock on Friday and expected people to be prepared by Monday at ten in the morning, unless there was some lengthy material for them to read.

Start the agenda by stating the ideal outcome of the meeting. In a weekly leadership meeting, the outcome may be pretty much the same every week: covering the priorities, discussing the red items, having a training on a specific topic for a specific purpose. There will be times, though, when situations arise that need to be tackled immediately and so that may take up a large part of the meeting or even the entire meeting time.

THE IDEAL MEETING

I believe the weekly meeting is *THE* most important meeting for people to grow as a team and for the organization to grow as a business. It must be treated as such. To me, the behavior each participant shows in and around this meeting highlights their desire to succeed. (To fully understand my meaning here, refer again to chapter 7 and John Wooden's definition of success.)

Let's step through a weekly meeting: You begin with Good News or Weekend Reports. You have an agenda that begins with checking in on the priorities. Use the red, yellow, or green approach to get a quick pulse on where everyone is with these priorities. If you get a "red," make a verbal note to get back to it. Once everyone's given you a red, yellow, or green, revisit those that need discussion. Whether or not they do is up to the owner.

Then go to training. Weekly and monthly team meetings should have a training component where you learn something new. It doesn't have to be a formal course. Training can be as simple as having the CFO show everyone how to read a balance sheet. Your leadership team should know how to do this, even if they're not directly involved in company finance. Another week, your CMO might do a quick training on the company's core customer, and what the marketing team has learned about them. Your leadership isn't going to know everything about every department, but they should have a good understanding of the most important concepts of each function of the business. Connect what they're learning to what they do in the business too, so they understand why they should care, and how they can use this new knowledge to improve their contributions to the business. Training, like everything else, should have a purpose.

During discussions in the meeting, everyone should have an equal say. Even if they don't have an opinion that differs from everyone else's, it's on you to ask them for their opinion. Allow them to contribute. They're thinking something about the topic at hand, and it could be more useful than they realize.

Resist the urge to brainstorm unless you have a specific purpose for doing so. Some people love brainstorming sessions, but they can take you down long-winded rabbit holes that lead nowhere and by the end of the meeting, nothing is accomplished.

The final part of the meeting can be Appreciations, a one-phrase closing, or a short analysis (three to five minutes) of how the meeting went with an eye on improving it next time.

I believe the weekly meeting is *THE* most important meeting for people to grow as a team and for the organization to grow as a business. It must be treated as such. To me, the behavior each participant shows in and around this meeting highlights their desire to succeed.

WEEKLY 1:1 CHECK-IN

Whether it's a daily huddle or a weekly, monthly, quarterly, or annual meeting, every time you get people together in your business, establish protocols and ground rules. Have a purpose and state it clearly. Following are my guidelines and best practices for running meetings that aren't boring and that people don't hate.

Most people need a frequent and light touch to feel valued and stay engaged. A great tool to do this is the Weekly 1:1. The Weekly 1:1 can be thirty minutes long but I prefer shorter ones—five to fifteen minutes—unless the team member requires more time for a specific topic, either personal or professional.

Here is what I recommend covering in each Weekly 1:1 Check-In:

1. **What is the key priority(ies) you are looking to achieve this week?**
2. **How can I help?** If they do not need help a few

weeks in a row and are consistently achieving outcomes, give them more challenging tasks. Learning is growing and growing is uncomfortable and filled with challenges. If they are not achieving outcomes yet not asking for your help, it is likely that they do not feel safe enough around you to do so.

3. **What did you love doing last week?** Ask them to reflect back to when the day or part of the day flew by. What were they doing? Keep a log of these tasks and activities for each person so you can provide them with more things to do that they love.

These three questions will go a long way to creating psychological safety and engagement and should take you no more than a few minutes each week to complete.

KEY TAKEAWAY

Meetings are expensive. The boring ones suck. Make the most of that time and don't allow them to be boring. Just cut all the boring stuff out that people can do on their own, like reading reports and looking at PowerPoints. Have the right people in the room and don't worry about not inviting people because they might get their feelings hurt. They are paid to be productive and want to be productive, not waste time in a meeting where they don't belong. If you don't think they will add any value or *they* don't think they will add any value, take them off the roster. Send them the notes.

Run the meeting efficiently and effectively with a solid agenda based on the ideal outcome, which should be about a priority that you've set for the business—a 3HAG, 1HAG, or QHAG—Three-Year, One-Year, or Quarterly Highly Achievable Goal. Prioritize your discussions in the meeting and make sure everyone has their say. If you've created the right environment, people will feel free to speak out, and call each other out. If someone says something that isn't true or if they go off on a tangent, other people in the room have the right to say something. The team leader isn't the only one keeping the meeting on track—everyone owns a piece of that.

If you change the way you do meetings, don't expect to hit your ideal outcome every time. If you only achieve it half the time those first few meetings, you're doing great. Practice and you'll get better.

You're going to feel really good the first time you do this and will wonder why you didn't start sooner. Your people will look forward to meetings. They'll have opportunities to contribute where they didn't before, and they'll have more time to get their work done by skipping those meetings they used to attend where they weren't needed. Those "meetings after the meeting" that they once depended on to get clarity, or where they shared their thoughts and opinions with a subset of the group because they didn't speak up or weren't given enough time to speak during the meeting, will disappear.

At this point, you've built your teams and you have a solid framework for a strategic execution system that involves making sure you know your customer and what they value. You set your priorities and created metrics to ensure you meet them. The only thing missing is a process that gets you more sales to your current core customers, and more new core customers. You do that with a sales playbook.

GET UP AND STRETCH

Supporting information, exercises, worksheets, and bonus content are available at *Further, Faster Resources*, https://catalystgrowthadvisors.com/catalyst-growth-advisors/further-faster-resources/, including the following:

- **Meetings with Purpose Sample Agendas**

CHAPTER 11

CREATE A SALES PLAYBOOK

There are only a few best ways to sell your products and services, not 50 or 100 or 1,000. Without a sales playbook that defines your best way, every single one of your sales reps is making up their own "best way".

—JACK DALY, *HYPER SALES GROWTH: STREET-PROVEN SYSTEMS & PROCESSES. HOW TO GROW QUICKLY & PROFITABLY* (PARAPHRASED)

Years ago, I took over a sales team at a startup. Some salespeople were consistently hitting their numbers but others were struggling. I worked with them to understand our customers and I spoke directly to many customers to learn what they valued from us. And I documented everything. The goal was to ensure that every one of my salespeople knew why people bought our products so they weren't wasting time on sales calls pitching features and benefits that didn't matter to our core customers.

I worked one-on-one with my team members to see where they were getting stuck on deals. All kinds of obstacles were hanging them up. Mostly, they didn't follow a process. They skipped key milestones and spent time on tasks that didn't need to be done. They thought they were on stage four of a sale, for instance, but they'd skipped stages two and three. Or they thought they were ready to close a deal when they hadn't even spoken with the decision-maker.

I learned that some of my people were very good at certain parts of the sale but less skilled in other parts. The funny thing was, they weren't even aware of it. I got them together in a meeting to talk about their individual talents and one person would say, "Heidi's really good at closing." Heidi didn't realize this, but everyone else in the room did. So I'd have Heidi step us through how she closed deals.

It turned out that everyone was good at something and some people were good at everything. We just needed to discover these skills, talk about them, and eventually document them so everyone could benefit from the team's collective skill set.

SALES SKILLS

When we did this, I didn't just ask the salesperson to explain their process. When you do something over and over again, it becomes so habitual that you don't even realize the tiny details of the process you've created. What I often did was interrogate them to help them get more detailed on their optimum steps in the process. It was the only way to figure out what each salesperson did that differentiated their process from everyone else's.

Other people started testing out these shared processes. Heidi's closing method might have to be tweaked for one salesperson because it didn't suit their personality, but the basics remained the same. As we tested them, we discussed ways to improve them.

I had established a framework for selling earlier in my career, and it worked with this team. We just had to make adjustments for the product, industry, and customer. Everything else was there, among my salespeople. They knew how to sell—we needed to get all that information out of them and make it accessible to the team.

We also had to uncover what people struggled with and talk about that openly. Sharing obstacles in front of your team members puts a salesperson in a vulnerable position. No one wants to admit that they're not very good at something they're being paid to do. You have to have that safe environment where people know they're not risking their career by speaking up about what they need from their team and the company. It's on you, the leader, to communicate to them that you don't expect anyone to know everything. That's not why you hired them. They're on your team because they're a great fit for the team and the company, and you know they can learn any skill they need to do their job well.

The more we learned about how to sell to our core customers, the more I documented, until I had developed a sales playbook. This became the gold standard for the sales team, so we were all selling basically the same way—the best way.

A playbook gets people on the same page, selling in a way that makes sense to your core customers. It instills purpose into your sales process. It drives the sales team further, faster toward an ideal outcome, and it clings to the core purpose and values of the business. It's a living, breathing document that reflects the overall strategy of the company, focusing time and attention on the right customers. Within the processes set forth in the playbook, you don't settle for letting customers pick you; you actively and purposefully pick your customers.

If you identify a customer who's not like your core customer base, only stray with good reason. You might bend a little, but you don't want to go two or three standard deviations from the core customer because the farther out you go, the more likely they'll be unhappy with you and you with them. Especially when they start pulling resources from the people you know will buy from you, year after year.

A lot of your sales will be repeat business—sales to your best customers. You know exactly who they are, what they value, and where to find them. This should be documented in a playbook that all your salespeople read and understand.

HOW TO WRITE A PLAYBOOK

There's no one best way to write a sales playbook because how you do it depends on your own skills. I'm very good at observing and interviewing people and noting patterns in their behaviors and responses. That was the technique I used to determine what worked best for my sales team.

Another way to gather this information is to have your salespeople write it. Say you have a team of ten. Split them into two teams of five people and task them with developing their own playbooks. Break it down into sections for each phase of the sales process and give them time every week to work on each section. The key thing here is that the team members can only talk to other members on their team about the playbook—they can't share between the teams. If they do that, it will limit their thinking and you want them to feel free to explore and share all their best ideas.

Then you share and compare the two playbooks. Discuss them and combine them into one. Use it for a month, with each team member noting what works and what does not, and then discuss the processes and modify them every month until you have a solid process for each phase.

By involving everyone in the development of the playbook, you've gleaned the best processes from your team. They've all contributed and can share joint ownership of it, so they're more likely to follow the practices. And when a new salesperson joins the team, you have a guide to hand them that gets them up to speed quickly, instead of fumbling through and learning as they go.

WHAT GOES IN YOUR SALES PLAYBOOK

The first section of your playbook is all about the company: your core values, core purpose, and vivid vision. You might want to add the function-organizational chart and the key process flow map (see chapter 4) so the sales team understands the context of their work and how it impacts the flow of money within the company.

The next section describes the market. Information here includes your core customers' problems, how you solve them, and what they value about your solution. Your marketing people will have more to add here, such as the key problems you are solving, the few main identifiers of your core customers' struggles, customer profiles, personas, demographics, psychographics, and the direct and indirect competition.

The third section of your playbook is a high-level methodology that describes how you address the market and acquire new customers. Explain how you create sales targets and benchmarks and describe your sales funnel. Other items to add here are the elevator pitch, frequently asked questions and how to address them, common objections and how to respond to them, and so on.

Reach out for help with sections of your playbook. The heads of sales and marketing will have plenty of information for you, and your sales team can fill in the rest.

The first version of your playbook won't be perfect and it isn't the final word on sales. Don't demand that everyone follow it to the letter. The sales team should test parts of it as needed, check the results, and report back. This is the fun part.

The hard part is discovering that you've been selling to

the wrong people and figuring out if you want to keep them as customers. These are conversations you'll have to have with the leadership team and with your salespeople.

Monitor the sales team and when you see someone struggling, talk to them again about what's hanging them up. Revisit the sales playbook and see if they're following it, because they are going to fall back into their old habits. That's what people do, and salespeople are no different. Coach them toward success, and if something in the playbook doesn't work for them, revise it so it does.

If as the leader, you find a trend where people are struggling with the same obstacles or there's a process that's not working, bring that to the sales meeting. Open the topic up for discussion and see if other salespeople have solved it. You might have four people who just can't seem to close a deal. Schedule a training session with Heidi (remember Heidi?) during a meeting to step people through her process, and have those salespeople talk to her about what works for them and what doesn't. They could be missing an important step, or they may have uncovered an obstacle that Heidi has never dealt with. Talk it out. Fix the process. Update the playbook.

If the salespeople are doing everything "by the book" during the close and they're still having problems, look at other stages. Their close rate may be off because they're not choosing the right customers to engage from the start, or they may not be nurturing the lead properly. They may not have identified the right decision-maker.

The sales playbook will make a vast difference for your sales team. Instead of having just a few great salespeople, you'll have everyone in various stages of selling well and getting better at it every day.

KEY TAKEAWAY

Write a playbook. Use it. Improve it. Without it, you are hoping Marketing and Sales are on the same page. You are assuming that your sales team is talking to the right customers, saying the right things, and closing the right deals. Without it, I can assure you, they are not.

When we act independently, we create our own version of actions that work for us. We gravitate toward our strengths, what we like to do, and what feels comfortable. Without a playbook, that's what every member of your sales team does. They'll believe their way is the best way too, even when it doesn't produce results. Convincing them that they don't know best is tricky, but if you've created a healthy team environment and hired people who believe in the company and what you're trying to accomplish, getting everyone on the same page won't be too difficult.

The message from you is this: "This is who we are. This is what we do. This is who our customers are. This is what they care about. This is how we solve their problem. This is how we answer the FAQs. These are the steps we take to go through the process. And this book isn't me, it's you—all of you. All of what we know and believe about our customers and the sales process that will take us further, faster."

Now that you know how to run a great meeting and how to put together a sales playbook, it's time to talk about sales and meetings—the sales meeting. Yes, that single meeting warrants its own chapter. It's that important. I can't tell you how many businesses I've worked with that have a "sales problem" when the problem isn't with their sales team at all—it's in their strategy, their sales process, and often right there in the sales meeting.

GET UP AND STRETCH

Supporting information, exercises, worksheets, and bonus content are available at *Further, Faster Resources*, https:// catalystgrowthadvisors.com/catalyst-growth-advisors/ further-faster-resources/, including the following:

• **Sales Playbook**

CHAPTER 12

‾‾‾‾‾‾‾‾

HAVE A WEEKLY SALES MEETING AGENDA

How you enter a space and how you leave a space is as important as what happens in the space.

—DICK AND EMILY AXELROD, *LET'S STOP MEETING LIKE THIS: TOOLS TO SAVE TIME AND GET MORE DONE*

I was talking with some of my colleagues about all the bad sales meetings we'd witnessed over the years. We'd seen it all:

- Meetings that started late
- Meetings that had no scheduled, hard stop
- Meetings with no agenda
- Long, meandering meetings to review the pipeline with no strategy and no short- or long-term goals

- Meetings that avoided discussing the most important issues, or that had no focus and no accountability
- Meetings where people walked away having learned absolutely nothing, more demotivated than when they walked into the meeting

This example of a real, worst-case scenario meeting came from my friend and colleague, Sales VP Kathy Yenke:

> The CEO is a very detail-oriented guy who, while he prepares for the meeting, expects his reps to be on standby. No one knows exactly when the meeting will begin or end. Their job is to show up when the meeting starts, and each one regurgitates every detail of every one of their deals, while all the other reps sit and listen—if they can stay awake. The CEO makes occasional comments but there is no real discussion, problem-solving, support, or follow-up.

Kathy's example beat out everyone else's and that's why I included it here. But despite how awful it sounds, there's actually something you can do that's much, much worse than running a bad meeting: not having one at all.

Want a surefire way to shorten your business career? Eliminate the weekly sales meeting. I can practically guarantee that you won't make your monthly targets without getting your sales team in a room every week.

But just having the meeting isn't enough. You have to do it right and make those meetings count—starting with the right agenda. The goal of the agenda is to get the information you need to predict the period (week, month, quarter, etc.) with a high level of accuracy *and* to continue to grow the level of your team. This will give you more time to focus on predicting the longer-term future of the business versus closing deals, going on excessive "ride withs," and having to pull a rabbit out of a hat every now and again to hit numbers, make payroll, and so on.

Your weekly meeting should include forecasting, learning, supporting and recognizing, and adjusting. Let's break it down and talk about what all that means.

FORECAST

The forecast has three parts: (1) in, (2) commit, and (3) upside. It's basically a status report with a forecast for the month plus any potential sales that aren't in the forecast. Each person on the sales team says where they are with their numbers for the month—what's already "in"—and what they're committing to by the end of the month. This assumes that the team is good at hitting what they commit to. When I led sales teams, I always had each person share these out loud each week in front of the entire team. The sales playbook and their personality type affect the accuracy of their forecast, so take all of that into consideration.

Do they follow the steps? Are they optimistic by nature or are they notorious sandbaggers? People are people and we all have our idiosyncrasies, but you want to identify and adjust for these variables as much as possible.

They should also briefly mention any potential upside. Once you have all the numbers from everyone, you can see how that cumulative number compares to the monthly target. Is it over? Under? By how much? If the in and commit do not add up to the right number, it is time to revisit the upside. What can you pull into the month, and what can you do to make that happen? Go around the room and get the details on each potential upside deal. Start with the biggest one that is furthest along in the process you have created in your Sales Playbook. If you can bring that in, maybe you won't need to count on the others. If not, move to the next one on the list, etc.

"Hey Sandy," you might say, "It sounds like there's an opportunity for you to pull in another 50K this month, which would make our team number. Talk to us about the deal: Who are you talking to, who's the decision-maker, and what needs to happen for them to pull the trigger? Help us understand it and we might have some ideas for you."

Once Sandy gives you the details, allow the team to discuss their ideas. No one person on the sales team knows everything—not even you—and you could be surprised by what other people come up with to close deals. They might know something about the client or about the product that you don't. Or they could have a creative way to shape the deal that makes it more attractive to the buyer. Maybe they read something online that morning about the industry itself that could change the client's mind and get them to a decision sooner. Who knows? You won't, unless you ask and let them respond.

The conversation should lead to a plan that Sandy can execute, so be sure to summarize that at the end of the discussion. The solution might be that you or someone else goes on the next call with Sandy, but don't let that be the end of it. Whatever you do has to raise the level of the team so they all learn from it and can leverage it going forward. And you can go on fewer sales calls, because that's not your main function in the company, right? Whoever is going on the call—Sandy, you, another salesperson—has to explain their plan, and after the call and at the next sales meeting, they have to give an update. What happened? Did the plan work or fail? Why?

You can see how the forecast leads to the next stage of the agenda: learning.

LEARN

Include a learning agenda item every week. What you discuss varies. You could invite someone in from the marketing, IT, engineering, tech support, or accounting departments to provide an overview of an upcoming event or campaign, application, product, or report. Just make sure it's something they need to know to be more efficient or productive—something that helps them and the team go further, faster. This isn't learning for learning's sake. There has to be a point to it.

I recommend starting with the weakest part of the sales cycle and teaching the team about that. Is it the opening, closing, the negotiation? Do that until 80 percent of the team is excellent at it and then move on. If you spend an inordinate amount of time on this topic, you may have a deeper problem. You have not hired well. That is a whole other problem.

Another topic for the learning session is a win report or a loss report. Choose a salesperson to present a deal they won or lost. Have them walk the team through the process they followed and how it aligns with the Sales Playbook. Encourage them to describe any barriers to the sale and how they overcame them. For a loss, they may have made assumptions about the customer. What is the upside to that—maybe taking on a customer that would never be happy—and how can they avoid doing the same thing again?

Review the playbook and discuss what's working and what isn't. Look at the various stages in the sales cycle and see if you can identify trends to focus on. You may be able to fix some problems within the sales team, but other problems may point to issues with marketing or product development. Your salespeople talk to the customer more than anyone in the company and their feedback is invaluable. Get them to talk in these learning sessions and pay attention to what they have to say.

SUPPORT, RECOGNIZE, AND APPLY

Wins usually come after weeks, months, or even years of work. Yet we tend to take them for granted. Think about all the effort that goes into an individual's and a team's successes. They need leadership to support them through the process, recognize their wins, and encourage them to talk about the losses too. There are lessons to be learned from both outcomes.

In my weekly sales meetings, I always made time to review the forecast and make sure everyone understood the income we expected to see and the potential upside. I asked people to talk about the struggles they were having, so we could support each other while leveraging the wisdom of the team to discover possible solutions.

You can easily formalize this process to ensure everyone

has a chance to lead the discussion. I would nominate a salesperson each week, for example, and tell them that they would have to present—in fifteen to twenty minutes and just a few slides—a recent loss or an account that they were having a hard time closing. Alternatively, they could talk through a win they had, and share their experience with the team.

In this way, the whole team benefited from every win and every loss. There were always new lessons to learn that could be applied, and some of what we learned found its way into the sales playbook. Even more importantly, it forced people to work together as a team. Instead of competing against each other, they taught one another, learned from each other, and shared in the struggles and the successes of every team member.

In the format I used, the slides had to answer these questions:

- What was the name of the account, project, or deal?
- What was the biggest challenge?
- What problem was the customer trying to solve?
- How were you helping them solve it? What products, services, etc.?
- Where did you get stuck?

If you've created a psychologically safe environment for

your people, they will feel comfortable enough to have this conversation with their peers.

Most people will talk about their wins, but some people will not. They are either too shy or just not comfortable talking about themselves, even in a positive way. They might be humble, or maybe they don't recognize the value of what they've accomplished. In these cases, the leader or the other team members have to do some of the crowing for them. It's not likely that a win was due to the efforts of just one individual, so talking about them is a great opportunity to call out everyone else who was involved—the "supporting cast of characters" who made the win possible.

Talking about wins and losses in meetings can be augmented with awards, too, and they don't have to be fancy or expensive. Something as simple as a plastic trophy or a stuffed animal that gets passed around each week, recognizing people on the team for their specific outcomes, brings levity to the group and makes the discussions more fun. Use your imagination and be consistent. Wins are seldom easy, and losses are difficult to discuss. They're both easier with recognition and support from your colleagues.

KEY TAKEAWAY

Sales is about execution. Execution is about habits and

discipline. Your sales meeting is THE place to demonstrate and build great habits and discipline. Take advantage of this great opportunity to build a great team that consistently meets or exceeds its numbers.

If you want to go fast, go alone. Be the superstar sales manager and close all the deals. If the business continues to grow, eventually you risk missing your number. While you can be the hero for a while, that's not your job. Your job is to make everyone else heroes. That's why you became a leader.

Done right, a sales meeting gives you a level of confidence that your team is going to hit that number and if they're not going to hit it, you know that in advance and have some time to do something about it. The sales meeting also raises the level of the team so that they're relying on you less and less to hit it.

Now that you've created an environment where teams thrive, hired the right people into those teams, developed a sales playbook that everyone's using, and you're running highly productive meetings, good results will follow. The right customers will want to buy the right products from you, and you'll start generating cash. Let's talk about that cash and why it's important.

GET UP AND STRETCH

Supporting information, exercises, worksheets, and bonus content are available at *Further, Faster Resources*, https://catalystgrowthadvisors.com/catalyst-growth-advisors/further-faster-resources/, including the following:

- **Customer -> Advocate Playbook**
- **Power of Moments Exercise**
- **Power of Moments One-Pager**

PART III

CASH IS KING

CHAPTER 13

////////////////////////////

TRUST CASH FIRST

Growth for the sake of growth is the ideology of a cancer cell.

—EDWARD ABBEY

During the late 1980s and early '90s, Dell was going out of business. They were growing so fast that they didn't have the cash to bankroll the demand for their product. They couldn't afford to pay their suppliers. When they sold computers, they lost cash. The company was essentially "growing broke."

Michael Dell hired Tom Meredith to solve the problem, and he changed the business model.

At the time, Dell maintained an inventory of computers that were shipped when a customer ordered one. Meredith suggested that they change the model to customize each order with the caveat that the customer pays for it up front, so Dell could pay their suppliers. The customer might have to wait for their computer, which was being custom-made, but Dell was getting their money and not having to dig into their own cash. Customers were willing to wait because they were getting a made-to-order item built to their needs and preferences.

Before going to this model, Dell had to pay their suppliers sixty-three days before they got any money from the customer. With this new system in place, they were getting paid thirty days before they had to pay their suppliers. They went from being a public company to buying back their business and going private, and then they bought EMC. They never could have had the money to do any of those things with their old model.

Other businesses have solved the cash problem by charging membership fees. Think Costco and Amazon, with its Prime membership service. This gives a company a huge influx of cash.

WHY WORRY ABOUT CASH?

So why should we care about cash? Isn't revenue where it's at? Well, not exactly. Revenue is great to talk about at parties, to brag about to your brother-in-law, or to share with a reporter on the growth of your company when asked. However, it is not a great metric for the health of your company. If revenue is what you're chasing, you're going to have problems eventually. Unless you're looking to sell your business or be acquired based on velocity, focusing on revenue isn't the same as money—*cash*—in the bank.

Cash is vital. It's the lifeblood of your business, which is why business leaders are always looking for more of it—even if they're not always looking in the right places. Cash is payroll. If you care about your employees and their families, payroll matters. Cash is fuel. Cash is what you need to invest back into your business and into your people to make your business better. Cash is not only how you survive the inevitable tough times, but also how you thrive. If you care about your business and your people, you have to invest in them. If you want to hang onto your customers and attract new ones, you have to *continuously* invest in them. That takes cash.

If you're a startup, unless you're looking to get bought in the near future, stop thinking about the amount of money you just raised. It might keep you going for a while, but at some point, you will have to *make* money. This is something business owners really need to think about: stop thinking about your business and its success in terms of revenue. Start focusing on increasing the amount of cash that you have so you can invest in your business and in the people driving your business.

CASH RESERVES

Every company needs a reserve of cash. Depending on the company, the amount ranges from one to six months of cash to keep your business going. Bill Gates has said that he wanted enough cash in Microsoft's reserves to keep the company afloat for an entire year, so that if they didn't make a single dollar for twelve months, they would still be able to pay all their expenses, their salaries, everything. They would survive.

Everyone hits a rough patch and you have to be able to get through them. Not having enough cash on hand is a poor excuse for a thriving company to go out of business.

DRIVING TOWARD PROFITS

Once you have enough cash in the bank, you can drive toward profit, but not profit for profit's sake. Look at making a profit to invest back in the business.

For most businesses, a good profit channel is between 10 and 15 percent net profit. If you're doing 10 percent, you're probably a solid business. From there, look at how you can improve efficiencies to increase the profit channel to 15 percent.

Next, reinvest that additional 5 percent to take your next

step of growth. It costs money initially to do that. You may have to lay out some cash to train people, or to purchase new hardware or software, or even build a factory. That initial cost might take your profits back down to 10 percent, but then the improvements you made allow you to gradually increase it. Once you're back at 15 percent, or whatever number you set for yourself, you look at what else you can do to improve your business.

You need cash to do all this.

HIDDEN CASH

During my workshops, I like to have the participants take part in exercises designed to get them thinking beyond their normal range of focus. One of my favorite activities is the Hidden Cash Exercise, which gets them to consider opportunities for creating more cash.

I tell the participants, "Did you know you have cash just sitting around in your business that you're not aware of?" When I say this, everyone looks at me like I have three heads. *Cash? Sitting around? I don't think so.* No one believes me. Leaders should know where all their cash is. So we do this exercise.

First, I explain the four business cycles that a business must complete to generate cash, which are derived from

Verne Harnish's "Cash Acceleration Strategies" exercise in his book, *Scaling Up*.[32]

1. Sales and marketing
2. Creating a product or service
3. Delivering or implementing the product or service
4. Getting paid for the product or service

Next, I ask everyone to estimate how long each of these cycles takes to complete, and then add those times up. "That," I say, "is how long it takes you to make money. You invest money upfront in that initial cycle but you don't get a dime back until the final cycle." Most leaders tell me it takes thirty, sixty, or ninety days, but I've had people tell me it takes their business a year to make money on that initial investment. Crazy, right?

The third step is to look closely at each cycle and think of ways to improve it. Typically, you can do this one of three ways:

1. Shorten the cycle.
2. Eliminate the most common mistakes in the cycle.
3. Improve the business model around the cycle.

I give everyone time to think about how they can improve

---

32   Verne Harnish, *Scaling Up: How a Few Companies Make It...and Why the Rest Don't* (Ashburn: Gazelles, 2014).

their four cash cycles one of these three ways, or any other way, which takes maybe twenty minutes. Then I ask them to share their best idea—one they can implement this year that will have a major impact. Since these leaders come from many different companies, I never ask them to share anything that's proprietary, but they usually have an idea that's so exciting, they're eager to share with everyone else in the workshop. I ask them to explain the cycle of cash it affects, the technique they're using to improve it, and the impact that improvement will have on their bottom line in the next year.

Are you surprised to hear that people often discover in this twenty-minute exercise that they could be saving tens of thousands of dollars? More than $100,000? That's exactly what happens. At that point in the exercise, by the way, they all agree they're getting a very good return on investment for the workshop (about 100x their investment!).

They didn't have to make anything or fire anyone to find that cash. This is money that's wasted due to inefficient cash cycles.

CINCINNATI CASH CONVERSION

At a peer-to-peer advisory meeting in Cincinnati, I took a group of businessmen through the Cash Acceleration

Strategies exercise. A guy from the design industry said that his cash conversion cycle was well over a year. Whenever he put a dollar into his business, he had to wait a year to get that dollar back.

He explained, "I'm in this design business, and when a customer comes to me, I do an intake and an analysis to gather information. Based on what I learn, I show them what I'm going to design. If they agree, I create it, but it might take a year to complete. Then once it's done and they approve the project, they pay me."

I asked him why he does it that way and he said, "If they don't like the final design, I don't want to take their money." I asked him how often someone doesn't like the design, and he said that out of roughly a hundred orders, a client had only turned down a completed design twice. For the 2 percent of all that business, he was holding back a lot of money that he could have been investing in the business or putting in the bank.

I asked him, "What could you do for your clients to get them to not worry about the final design and be willing to pay you upfront?" He said that he would be willing to give his clients a money-back guarantee if the design didn't meet their criteria. If he didn't deliver as promised, they would have the right to cancel the order and get a full refund.

This solution would allow him to take in millions of dollars when the order was placed, instead of waiting a year to recoup his investment and make a profit. This might seem obvious to some people, but every day, business owners don't see these solutions because they don't even look for them. Instead, we get caught up in the tyranny of the moment and the status quo. "Busy is good," we tell ourselves, but if you're running the business, busy is not good. To run the business smarter, you need time to think about how you could be running it better—that's your job.

FORECAST FOR CASH, NOT REVENUE

Most companies forecast how much revenue they want to make and go after that goal. A better method is forecasting how much cash you want to add to your existing reserves.

Figure out how much cash you want at the end of the year, subtract what's in your coffers, and make the difference your goal. Then decide how much revenue you need to generate to hit your target. You should already know how much revenue you need, after expenses, taxes, and anything else that costs you revenue, to get a set amount of cash, so use that formula and figure it out. That will tell you how big you need to be—how much revenue and profit you need to generate in a year—to have your forecasted cash in the bank.

You need that cash to grow in whatever way you've defined for your business, and you need to invest in ways that you've defined to get there. The other option is to borrow money, which isn't an awful idea but it's not preferred either. Borrowed money has to be paid back, which means drawing money out of your cash reserves on a regular basis and possibly ceding some control to a third party.

Try to fund your business yourself, but look at other options when it makes sense. If you need to accelerate your business quickly but you don't have the cash for the necessary investments, consider a short-term loan. Just look at the numbers and make sure your investment allows you to generate enough additional revenue to pay it back quickly.

FOCUS ON THE MONEY

Of all the information in all the documents, reports, and spreadsheets you look at, cash is the only line item that will not lie to you. You either have cash or you don't. You can make up profit. You can spend less and move expenses around. You can lower your salary and show a "profit" but in the end, if you're being honest about what your business is worth, you have to look at the going rate for yourself and your leadership team and take that off the bottom line. Suddenly, you're not profitable.

You have to focus on cash, and four key tasks will help you do that.

GET A WEEKLY CASH FLOW STATEMENT

First, ask your CFO to send you a cash flow statement every single week. The statement should answer these questions:

- How much cash did we start the week with?
- How much cash did we generate in the week?
- How much cash did we spend in the week?
- How much cash is left?

Most weeks, you won't see anything different or particularly interesting. You'll put the statement aside and after enough weeks like this, you may stop looking at it altogether. Don't. Look for those occasional statements where you end up with twice as much cash as usual, or half as much. Find out why. What happened?

If you're making $1,000 to $10,000 a week and then one week you make $500 or $15,000, look at what changed. Track your cash conversion cycle and see if something changed. Was there a change in production, sales, or delivery? Did the billing process change? You need to know this.

If your weekly cash flow statement is long and complicated, ask your finance person to pull out those four numbers and put them at the top of the report. Because no matter how busy you are and how many reports you have to look at, you need to know that information every week.

ESTABLISH WORKING CAPITAL

Second, establish working capital. Have some cash in reserves. How much depends on your business, and it can be hard to put an exact number on it. But figure out how much money you would need to keep the business going if no money was coming in, and bank it. This might be three months, six months, or a year's worth of payroll, expenses, and whatever else you spend money on to run the place. This way, if there is ever an issue that prevents you from generating revenue, you'll have enough cash to keep the business going while you fix the problem. For a small business, a couple of months' worth of cash might be enough, but for large enterprises, it might be wise to have a whole year of cash set aside.

That working capital is the first place you should invest money in your profit channel. Set a cash goal for your reserve and meet it before you invest in anything else. The money can be invested to make money for you but do so wisely, with no risk. Revisit your working capital periodically—at least once a year—because as your business grows, it costs more to run and so your reserves should reflect that growth. Expenses go up, salaries go up, rent goes up. All those increases should be accounted for.

DECIDE WHERE TO INVEST THE REST

Third, once you've filled your cash coffer, look at where else you should invest your cash. You can invest in your people, in your infrastructure, and anywhere else that would make your company better for your people and your customers.

REPEAT THE CASH CONVERSION CYCLE EXERCISE

Fourth, repeat the cash conversion cycle exercise every quarter or every couple of quarters.

Involve the leadership team in these activities too. Make them aware of them. Put someone in charge of the line items on your P&L statement. Your Head of Sales might own revenue and your Head of Operations might own expenses. So when you sit down to talk about what's going well and what isn't, you have someone to address it. They should be looking for anomalies that point to issues and opportunities and bringing them to the team for discussion.

SEVEN LEVERS

Your cash flow tells a story about your business. Think of it within the context of what Alan Miltz of Cash Flow Story calls the "seven levers" of your business:[33]

1. Price
2. Volume
3. Cost of Goods Sold
4. Accounts Receivable
5. Accounts Payable
6. Inventory
7. Overhead

These seven layers drive profit or take away profit from your business. Understanding how changing one of them affects the others and in turn, your bottom line, can help you make decisions that drive profit. You might be able to raise prices enough that it doesn't have a negative effect on the volume of goods sold. Or you may be able to lower prices to the point that you sell enough additional volume that your cost of goods sold per item decreases and you make more profit. What would happen if you collected money a few days sooner and paid your suppliers a few days later? Would people be okay with that? How much money would that make for you? Work with your team to examine each of the seven levers. Look at how moving one of them affects the others and in turn, profit.

---

33   Alan Miltz, cashflowstory.com.

Many leaders never do this. They don't consider raising prices until they have to, for fear they'll lose business. They look at what the competition's charging and think that all they have to compete on is price. Don't assume your competitors know more than you do. They're probably looking at *your* prices.

TRUST CASH FIRST

To repeat this chapter's epigraph: *Growth for the sake of growth is the ideology of a cancer cell.* The result can be compared to what happens when you focus on growing revenue for the sake of growing revenue. Instead, focus on cash and then figure out how much revenue you need to generate that much cash.

Cash allows you to run your business well over the long term. It allows you to hire and reward your best people and make strategic bets on the business. When you focus on the amount of cash that you need to grow, you grow in a much healthier way with less stress on yourself and all the stakeholders in your business, including your employees, suppliers, and customers. To get further, faster, understand how you generate cash and how to generate more cash sooner, as opposed to creating revenue.

As the business owner, it's on you to make this happen. That means avoiding the flawed assumption that if you grow the top line, the bottom line will come along. You can grow your top line by bringing in a lot of customers, but if you bring on the wrong kinds of customers, the benefits will be short-lived. Customers that you can't satisfy will not be happy with the product and they will be calling you, putting a drain on your people and ultimately sucking cash from your business. When people are buying and you're making revenue, you're not thinking about how this will affect your business six months or a year from now. But you have to think that way to survive.

GRAY MATTERS: SHORT-TERM SURVIVAL

Short-term thinking is a human flaw that served us well for survival but doesn't work so well when it comes to building a sustainable business. Many years ago, we had to be on the move to survive. We went where the food was, where the herd was. We were always in search of calories for energy because we didn't know when we'd eat again. So we might get a little fat, but we'd lose the fat when food was scarce. We're still wired this way, but with so much access to food, we just get fat. And we still have that short-term mentality.

We like short-term rewards because this is how our brains evolved. Think about how that mentality manifests itself in the stock market. Companies aren't rewarded for long-term investment. Like Milton Friedman says, "It's all about the shareholder."

If a company makes the shareholder happy with short-term results, they look good. But they often do so at the expense of long-term performance.

That drive for short-term results kills businesses. The average lifespan of a company on the Fortune 500 used to be around seventy-five years; now it's closer to fifteen! Only sixty businesses of the 1955 Fortune 500 were still on that list in 2017.[34]

It is better to focus on the long term. Companies that embrace so-called "conscious capitalism" have proven that, in the long run, it is better to invest in the business for the sake of *all* the stakeholders: team, customers, partners, suppliers, society, and the environment. According to a 2013 article, eighteen publicly traded (conscious capitalism) companies out of twenty-eight outperformed the S&P 500 index by a factor of 10.5 over the years 1996-2011.[35] People who have been recognized as conscious capitalists include leaders and former leaders of companies like Starbucks, The Motley Fool, Panera Bread, Whole Foods Market, and Ben & Jerry's.[36]

---

34 Mark J. Perry, "Fortune 500 firms 1955 v. 2017: Only 60 remain, thanks to the creative destruction that fuels economic prosperity," *AEI.org*, October 20, 2017, aei.org/carpe-diem/fortune-500-firms-1955-v-2017-only-12-remain-thanks-to-the-creative-destruction-that-fuels-economic-prosperity/.

35 Tony Schwartz, "Companies that Practice 'Conscious Capitalism' Perform 10x Better," *Harvard Business Review*, April 4, 2013, https://hbr.org/2013/04/companies-that-practice-conscious-capitalism-perform.

36 "Inaugural 'Heroes of Conscious Capitalism' Honorees Announced," *consciouscapitalism.org*, https://www.consciouscapitalism.org/blog/heroes-of-conscious-capitalism-2017-class.

KEY TAKEAWAY

Growth sucks cash. Build your business to support your cash needs first. Every other business metric is set and achieved in service of your cash plan.

Revenue is vanity, profit is sanity, cash is king.

—SOURCE UNKNOWN

Although we're wired for short-term survival, we can make conscious decisions to go against our wiring and do things differently. If you're just looking to flip your company, a short-term strategy might make sense. But if you want your business to endure, you have to adopt a long-term mentality.

Revenue is fine for bragging at parties and talking to the press. Revenue gives the impression that you're doing great. But cash is much, much more important—it's the jet fuel of your business. Revenue might move you toward your destination, but without cash, you'll run out of fuel, and maybe crash, before you get there.

GET UP AND STRETCH

Supporting information, exercises, worksheets, and bonus content are available at *Further, Faster Resources*, https:// catalystgrowthadvisors.com/catalyst-growth-advisors/ further-faster-resources/, including the following:

- **Cash Conversion Cycle Exercise (Cash Acceleration Strategies)**

CONCLUSION

What I found over the years is the most important thing is for a team to come together over a compelling vision, a comprehensive strategy for achieving the vision, and then a relentless implementation plan.

—ALAN MULALLY

In business and in life, few things truly do matter, but those that do, matter tremendously. The key to effective leadership and running a successful business is figuring out what few things truly matter. Identify those few things that truly matter to your team and your customers. Strip away the things that matter less so you can pursue perfection for the few things that truly matter.

As a leader, your job is no longer about running the ship, but understanding the direction of the seas and the impact of the wind. To navigate, not steer. To figure out where you are going over the next few years with such clarity and vivid detail that you describe the future as if you have already arrived.

Your team is thirsty for this. They want to know, "Where are we going? What is the North Star, the Core Destination, the BHAG? Where are we headed and how will we recognize it when we arrive?"

To do this, you must, as quickly as possible, fire yourself from the day-to-day. Make yourself useless so you can focus on the essential. Greg McKeown says that essentialism is not about how to get more things done; it's about how to get the right things done. This doesn't mean just doing less for the sake of less either; it's about making the wisest possible investment of your time, attention, and energy to operate at your highest point of contribution by doing only what is essential.

> "...The faster and busier things get, the more we need to build thinking time into our schedule. And the noisier things get, the more we need to build quiet reflection spaces in which we can truly focus... You cannot overestimate the unimportance of almost everything."[37]

To go further, faster, it is essential to ignore the siren song

---

37 John C. Maxwell, *Goodreads*, https://www.goodreads.com/quotes/154254-you-cannot-overestimate-the-unimportance-of-practically-everything.

of the moment's tyranny, the trivial but familiar, and the mink holes (which are really just rat holes that feel warm and comfortable).

The key is to find out what truly matters to your customers and team members. Create the space and time to think, to ponder, to ask questions of childlike curiosity and to create the environment so the ones nearest the problem have the authority and the framework to make the best possible decision on their own. Freeing you up to create and continually validate or update the framework that drives the business so that if you took a month-long vacation, from the outside, no one would even notice you were gone.

Throw out the rule book. Most were designed for the 1 percent while pissing off the other 99 percent anyway. As Simon Sinek says, "Rule books tell people what to do. Frameworks guide people how to act. Rule books insist on discipline. Frameworks allow for creativity." I personally like the rule book that has one rule. "Do what is best for the company and the customer." With a solid framework and the right trusted team in place, you will only need this one rule.

With so much change coming at an increased pace, leaders have to get out of the way and allow the capable, knowledgeable, and trusted team to take care of the business. You hired these great people, after all! As Richard Branson says, "You have to train people so well that they can leave and treat them so well that they never want to." When you have extraordinary confidence in your highly skilled and engaged teams, they perform extraordinarily.

Peter Drucker taught us that effective executives do not make a great many decisions. They concentrate on what is important. They try to make *the* few important decisions on the highest level of conceptual understanding. They try to find the constants in a situation, to think through what is strategic and generic rather than "solve problems."

SPARKING SOMETHING DIFFERENT

"Sparking" something different was the genesis of what eventually would become this book. In the introduction, I told you that the most successful leaders create their future. I shared a story about one of my own experiences, setting an organization on a new and better path, taking it further, faster. Let me tell you a little more about how that story played out:

As GM of a SAAS email hosting company many years ago, I was striving to create greater cohesion among my leaders and also the entire team of about sixty people. The need for this creation, as in most change, was born out of necessity. The day I took over as GM, we suffered a catastrophic infrastructure failure resulting in the loss of hundreds of customers within a week. It turns out that people get pretty angry when they cannot send or receive email for an extended period of time.

We were a technology company but our business was primarily a service. Since we were in a highly competitive space, one way to differentiate beyond technology was to provide tremendous and reliable service. To do this, I wanted to focus everyone on providing and recognizing exemplary service—to catch someone doing something right. Among the practices we put in place was a process where you could Spark another team member. When anyone noticed another team member giving extraordinary service to a customer or helping another member out to support a customer in an extraordinary way, they could Spark that person. Anyone could do this: no management approval required. When someone was Sparked, an email was sent out to the entire company describing why that person deserved mention. They also got $50 from the company—immediately and in cash.

Further, at our all-hands, monthly meeting, those who were Sparked that month were acknowledged again. The person who Sparked them re-read the email that was sent describing the extraordinary service. We asked each person, if they felt comfortable, to come up to the front of the room to receive a blue ribbon they could hang on their wall or cube. Much to my pleasant surprise, these ribbons were prominently displayed in the recipient's space for all to see.

Lastly, the senior leadership team picked one person to win the monthly Spark Award, which was dinner for two on the company and, at the end of the year, one person was chosen from the previous twelve monthly winners received a weekend away for two on the company.

This process, among other changes (including fixing the original technical problem) had a great impact on employee engagement, customer satisfaction scores, and overall revenue and profit. Our customer satisfaction scores went from 2.9 out of 5 (58 percent) when I took over as GM to 4.6 out of 5 (92 percent) in less than a year. We went from a catastrophic event to a highly functioning, cohesive, and productive organization nearly doubling revenue within two years. Even though revenue went up considerably, we only needed to hire a small number of new team members since productivity also went up considerably with essentially the same team.

TAKE THE NEXT STEP

There's a Better Way to Go Further, Faster

There is a better way that gets you further, faster and is easier and more sustainable. The better way is to focus on the few things that truly matter. This change starts with you as the leader, focusing not on yourself, but the two most important constituencies in your business—your people and your customers—in that order.

If you are dissatisfied as a leader and ready to challenge the status quo, establish a compelling vision as your first step to go further, faster. Any leader, no matter how long they've been in business, can start the first step to spark change by asking one simple question, as Cameron Herold shares in his prescriptive book *Vivid Vision*: "What is the ideal outcome I envision for this business and the stakeholders it serves?"

Write your answer clearly and simply. This is your vision, not a watered-down consensus-based vision statement. This is your manifesto. Your idea of an ideal future state.

Once you have a solid first draft, share it with your team to make sure they understand it fully and make changes if necessary, for clarity. Then, and only then, weave it into everything you do from hiring to exiting to growing and to serving.

That will be the first step of going further and faster than you ever thought possible. I will join you on the journey for this and what I believe are the other key initial steps to transform your business, your life, and the lives of those around you to be exceptional. I also look forward to you helping me to fulfill my core purpose, my why: simplified servanthood. To spend each working moment helping to create a society that is compassionately productive through having enlightened leaders focus on the few things that truly matter to their customers and teams.

Let's go. We've got this. You've got this. Of that, I have no doubt.

APPENDIX

BILL'S SUGGESTED READING AND LISTENING LIST

I read about fifty books every year and those that I believe are worth your time and effort—that hold the best nuggets of wisdom within their pages—are listed on my webpage under "Bill's Suggested Reading List" at https:// catalystgrowthadvisors.com/catalyst-growth-advisors/ resources/. These are practical, actionable, evidence-based books, versus hypothetical or theoretical tomes listed to impress. The knowledge in these books—and podcasts—works for almost every business and industry.

You can sign up for my updated list, which I send every six months, by subscribing to Bill's Blog. Just enter your email address in the top right corner of that page and select "Follow." The book list is my most popular email because people want to know what's worth reading, and they want recommendations from a reliable source. I also blog twice a month about the books, to provide insight on what I found most useful.

ACKNOWLEDGMENTS

Thanks to my family—Renata, Maggie, and Julie—for your support in my recent career switch and book project.

Thank you to those great leaders I have worked with and learned from over the years: Gordon Hoffstein, Bob Cramer, Keith Cupp, Patty Flynn, Paul Esdale, Blair Heavey, Verne Harnish, Gail Goodman, Rick Houpt ("mink hole" man), and Paul Chisholm.

Thank you to those who took the time to write and put their names on this book with their blurbs: Cameron Herold, Ari Weinzweig, Shannon Susko, Ken Estridge, Dave Baney, Harlan Geiser, Elizabeth Crook, and Jonathan Goldhill.

Thank you to all those who helped in the formation of this book and supporting materials: Doug Diamond, Harlan Geiser, Renata Aylward, Bruce Eckfeldt, Kevin

Lawrence, Scott Livingston, Lisa Vitale, Willow Volante, Tommy Farrell, Joe Marchand, Kris Holloway, Rich Hendgen, Paul Bierden, Dustin Campbell, Dr. Brad Weiss, Phil Muscatello, Jeff Palm, Nick Bryngelson, Craig Palli.

A special thanks to Susan Joy Paul, who was instrumental in the forming of this book. I literally could not have done it without her.

Thank you to my clients and peers who helped to make this book and my final career possible. Represented by each leader: Dustin Campbell, Phil Muscatello, Erik Waters, Jeff Palm, Nick Bryngelson, Rich Webb, Kris Holloway, Rich Kurtzman, Dr. Brad Weiss, Richard Hendgen, Brad Mindich, Lisa Vitale, Doug Barth, Doug Reeves, Dmitriy Peregudov, Brian Farrell, Tommy Farrell, Joe Marchand, Chris Macek, Lisa Foulger, Bruce Eckfeldt, Michael Synk, and Max Kozlovsky.

Finally, thanks to those thought leaders past and present who have helped to shape my thinking over thirty years: Andy Grove, Simon Sinek, Amy Edmondson, Bob Moesta, Clayton Christensen, Edward Deming, Greg McKeown, Pat Lencioni, David Rock, Verne Harnish, Shannon Susko, Marcus Buckingham, Rory Vaden, Ashley Goodall, Richard Koch, Peter Drucker, Bill Campbell, Jonathan Haidt, Chip and Dan Heath, Steve Blank, Cindy Alvarez, Dan Ariely, Cameron Herold, Dave Snowden, and Ari Weinzweig.

ABOUT THE AUTHOR

BILL FLYNN has more than thirty years of experience working for and advising hundreds of companies, including startups, where he has a long track record of success. He's had five successful outcomes, two IPOs, and seven acquisitions, including a turnaround during the 2008 financial crisis. Bill is also a multi-certified growth coach, has a Certificate with Distinction in the Foundations of NeuroLeadership and is a Certified Predictive Index Partner. He speaks around the country at various industry events and peer advisory organizations such as Vistage and YPO. Away from work, he is an avid reader and athlete, and enjoys volunteering locally. When he is not off cheering on his collegiate-champion daughter, Bill lives in Sudbury, Massachusetts, with his wife, dog, cat, and four chickens.

Contact Bill on his website at www.catalystgrowthadvisors. com, on LinkedIn at https://www.linkedin.com/in/ billflynnpublic, or by email at bill@catalystgrowthadvisors. com.